UNIVERSITY OF NORTH CAROLINA
STUDIES IN THE ROMANCE LANGUAGES AND LITERATURES
Number 66

GONZALO FERNÁNDEZ DE OVIEDO Y VALDÉS

GONZALO FERNÁNDEZ DE OVIEDO Y VALDÉS

AN ANNOTATED BIBLIOGRAPHY

BY

DAYMOND TURNER

Published with the Cooperation of
THE UNIVERSITY OF DELAWARE

CHAPEL HILL
THE UNIVERSITY OF NORTH CAROLINA PRESS

DEPÓSITO LEGAL: V. 3.140 - 1966

ARTES GRÁFICAS SOLER, S. A. - JÁVEA, 30 - VALENCIA (8) - 1966

ACKNOWLEDGEMENT

The author wishes to make public acknowledgement of his indebtedness to a number of persons who have contributed to the success of this undertaking. Special mention must be accorded to Professors Sterling A. Stoudemire and Sturgis E. Leavitt of the University of North Carolina, the former for fostering his interest in the literature of exploration and the latter for introducing him to Spanish-American bibliography. Professor John E. Keller of the same institution has also been most helpful in his editorial advice.

At the University of Delaware Dr. John M. Dawson, Director of Libraries, and the staff of the Morris Library, particularly Miss Ruth Alford, Reference Librarian, have been most helpful. Support in the acquisition of materials has been received from the University of Delaware Library Associates and the Faculty Committee on Research. And special tribute is due the Faculty Committee on Publications for assistance in producing the present edition.

To all of the foregoing and to many others who, for reasons of space, must go unmentioned I wish to express my sincere gratitude, accepting full personal responsibility for any errors which may follow.

DAYMOND TURNER

INTRODUCTION

None of the entries under «Oviedo» in the 1963 edition of *Encyclopedia Britannica* refer to the writer Gonzalo Fernández de Oviedo y Valdés who seems to have last appeared in that venerable reference work in 1952. And the entry under his name in the 1962 edition of *The Encyclopedia Americana* is brief and inaccurate. Despite the foregoing, in the winter of 1965, more than four hundred years after his death, more of his works are currently available in print than was the case at any time during his life. Menéndez Pelayo, while admitting his lack of poetic talent, includes him among the earliest Spanish-American poets, and, as I have pointed out elsewhere, he is the author of what is probably the first novel written in the Americas in Spanish. Moreover, the writings of this sixteenth century Spanish polygraph, who was personally acquainted with so many of the prominent men of his day and who spent nearly half of a long and varied career in the New World, remain as indispensable resources for the study of certain aspects of the reign of Ferdinand and Isabel and the beginnings of the European settlement of the Western Hemisphere.

In preparation for my forthcoming translation and edition of Oviedo's *Historia general y natural de las Indias...* I have been struck by the lack of any readily available listing of the various editions of his published works in the several languages into which they have been translated, a reasonably complete census of extant manuscripts, or any study, which, by relating his works to that of others would indicate his place in the development of Spanish literature or reflect the scope of his influence on the historiography of Spain and the New World.

No completely satisfactory biography of Oviedo exists. The numerous authobiographical allusions in his published works are marred by distortion of emphasis and artful omission. Amador de los Rios' study, contained in his introduction to the 1851-55 edition of the *Historia general...* and long accepted as standard, is now dismissed as an inaccurate panegyric. Within the past decade there have been a number of valuable contributions, most notably those of Pérez de Tudela, in his Introduction to the 1959 edition of the *Historia general...*, and of Peña and Otte which will be entered in the appropriate places below.

Nevertheless, certain facts of his career seem to be reasonably well established. He was born in Madrid of Asturian ancestry, in the year 1478. He is curiously reticent about his immediate family. But his father was one Miguel de Sobrepeña, a servant in the household of a homonym of the future chronicler, Gonzalo Fernández de Oviedo. His mother was a Juana de Oviedo.

Around 1490 he entered the service of the young Duke of Villahermosa, nephew of Ferdinand the Catholic, as a page. Some three years later, possibly at Barcelona, he joined the household of Prince John, only son of the Catholic Sovereigns, in the capacity of *mozo de cámara*. His duties, which he describes for us in detail in his *Libro de la cámara* appear to have been those of a sort of master of the wardrobe with responsibility for maintaining an inventory of his young master's clothing and insuring its safekeeping in that peripatetic establishment.

His rank was such as to preclude any thought of friendship with his illustrious patron, but here, as in the household of Villahermosa, he was able to observe near at hand many of the notable events and personalities of his time. And following the custom established by his father, he made and preserved memoranda of those personalities and events. This employment was terminated by the death of the prince in October 1497, but he remained with the court for approximately a year thereafter.

In the year 1499 Gonzalo passed to Italy, where, he was to serve a succesion of noble patrons, and also serve *a sueldo de guerra*. Given his experience, this last does not necessarily imply active combat. He more likely served as a sort of supply clerk or quartermaster sergeant. He was in Rome in the jubilee year 1500, later entered the service of the «young Queen Juana» of the royal house of Naples in a capacity very like that in which he had followed prince John. He accompanied her into exile in 1501.

From Italy he brought a knowledge of the Tuscan language and a collection of books, some of which were to remain by him till his old age. His activities upon his return to Spain are not clearly established. He seems to have followed the court for a period and to have worked both as a notary for the Inquisition and as a notary public in Madrid. Around 1502 he married Margarita de Vergara who, he tells us, was «the most beautiful woman in the kingdom of Toledo.» Three years later she was to die after a difficult childbirth which had turned her golden hair white in a single night.

A son, whom Peña believes to be illegitimate, was born to Oviedo in 1509. In the same year or the next he was to marry Isabel de Aguilar who would accompany him to the Indies and who would die in Santa María in 1522. In 1512 he enlisted as secretary in the abortive expedition against Naples headed by Francisco Hernández de Córdoba, «el Gran Capitán.»

Lope Conchillos, Secretary for Indian Affairs, designated the future chronicler as his deputy in the expedition of Pedrarias Dávila to Castilla del Oro, confirming this with the award of a rich portfolio of appointments. To these, before the fleet sailed on April 11, 1514, was added the post of *Veedor* or inspector of the gold foundries of that overseas possession. The armada reached Santa María la Antigua del Darién on June 30, and the new royal official entered zealously on the discharge of his manifold responsibilities which within ten months, according to Otte, had produced a profit of some 250,000 maravedis.

For reasons that are not entirely clear, despite his pious protest that it was to inform the King of the maladministration and abuses of Pedrarias, he then decided to return to Spain. En route, he stopped over at Santo Domingo where he received letters attesting to his value as a witness to matters on Tierra Firme. In December 1515 he was able to see the ailing King Ferdinand at Plasencia and received permission to visit his family in Madrid.

Upon obtaining news of Ferdinand's death in January 1516, Gonzalo set out for Flanders to inform his successor. A rough, stormy voyage from La Coruña finally came to an end at Dover, whence his ship crossed to Calais and thence he proceeded to Brussels. Chancellor Sauvage referred him to the regents of Castile. But his reception there by Cardinal Cisneros in the autumn of 1516, was equally chilly. Pérez believes that the following two and one-half to three years were spent in writing and renewing and strengthening old ties with his erstwhile protector Conchillos.

During the early part of 1519 he was in Valencia, superintending the printing of *Claribalte*... the novel of chivalry which he tells us was written «estando yo en la India». Then came his famous confrontation with Las Casas at Barcelona. In the debate on Indian policy the views of the Bishop of Chiapa would prevail, but our Veedor did not in the meantime neglect his own interests. Between June and December of that year he obtained confirmation of some of his former offices and an impressive list of new appointments.

In May of 1520, accompanied by his second wife, two children, and eight servants he set out on a second journey to Darién. After a rapid crossing they reached Santo Domingo, where they spent a week, dropping anchor at Santa María la Antigua on June 24. There Oviedo learned of the death of Sosa whom he had expected to succeed Pedrarias. Nevertheless, he did not at once renew his quarrel with the «Justiciador» who shortly removed to the recently founded city of Panamá on the Pacific side of the Isthmus.

This second residence in the New World was to last for slightly more than three years. Our author built a fine house at Santa María, in which, as he tells us, a prince might have been comfortably lodged. His duties as royal offical entailed considerable travel about the Isthmus, he engaged in various trading ventures with the Indians about the Gulf of Urabá, obtained what was nearly a monopoly of the pearl trade, and as an officer of the municipality struggled (not without self-interest) to prevent the complete abandonment of Santa María la Antigua following transfer of the administrative center to the other side. At the end of October 1522 he returned from Panamá with an appointment as lieutenant of Governor Pedrarias to find his wife seriously ill. She and the two children of this second marriage were to be buried in Darién. He became embroiled in open disagreement with his old antagonist Pedrarias and was replaced as lieutenant by Bachiller Corral. He also quarreled with a number of other prominent citizens of Darién and an almost successful attempt to assassinate him was made as he stood talking at the door of the church. He can not have received the capitulations countersigned by his patron Cobos on June 26, 1523 granting him the governorship of Cartagena and trading concessions in that area (upon fulfillment of certain conditions which he never carried out) before his departure for Spain on July 3 of that year.

His embarkation was made secretly and on pretext of being en route to Panamá. Instead he went to Cuba where he was cordially entertained by Governor Diego Velázquez for two or three weeks. From Cuba he crossed to Hispaniola and in Santo Domingo arranged to return to Castile with a group of three ships commanded by Admiral Diego Columbus, who invited the Inspector of Gold Foundries in Tierra Firme to accompany him aboard the flagship. Shortly before setting sail, after what must have been a brief courtship, Oviedo married one Catalina de Ribafrecha, September 16, 1523. Peña believes that the bridegroom acquired property in Santo Domingo at this time and that his natural son, Francisco, remained there with the bride of a few weeks. It is not clear whether his wife and son joined him on the Mainland on his return from Spain in 1526, or whether they were to remain overseeing his interests on Hispaniola until his return to that island for a more protracted stay in 1532.

On this voyage of 1523 Oviedo was to remain less than three years in the peninsular homeland. For much of this period he was engaged in following a peripatetic court and Council of the Indies from Burgos to Victoria, from Victoria to Burgos, from Burgos to Valladolid, laboring to secure the removal of Pedrarias a governor of Castilla del Oro, a result obtained with the support of other malcontents in August of '25, giving advice on the treatment of Indians, and seeking privileges for his friends and himself. Among these latter was a renewal of the license to settle Cartagena on even more favorable terms than those granted in the capitulations of 1523. His *Respuesta a la epístola moral del almirante...* may date from this visit home, if we can explain away the reference to the *Quincuagenas...* (finished in late 1554) in the title, but in view of content, his *Relación de lo sucedido en la prisión del rey Francisco...* could hardly have been composed prior to his third return to Castile (ca. 1530), even though he must have seen the French King and witnessed some of the events described on this earlier trip. He was in Toledo in early 1526, where he obtained a license to print a Spanish translation of *Il corvaccio...* of Giovanni Boccacio under the title *Laberinto de amor*. It is not known whether this version ever saw print, but in the same year he superintended the printing of his *De la natural historia de las Indias* which was issued at the author's expense by the Toledan printer Remon de Petras on February 15. In the spring of 1526 he set out from Seville in the party of Pedro de los Ríos who had been selected to succeed Pedrarias as governor of Castilla del Oro.

Their flotilla reached Nombre de Dios on the last day of July, thence Ríos and his party crossed to Panamá to await the return of the Justiciador from Nicaragua for his *residencia*.

Having accepted a compromise settlement of his claims against the ex-governor, Oviedo, towards the end of 1526, or the beginning of '27, moved to León de Nagrando in Nicaragua, where Diego López de Salcedo, whose wife was a cousin of Catalina de Ribafrecha, was exercising authority as governor, ignorant of the fact that that post had been awarded in March of 1526 to his ancient foe Pedrarias Dávila. Our Inspector apparently planned to establish residence there, for once again he had built a costly house. The arrival of the governor-designate around Easter of 1527 caused an upheaval in the affairs of the colony, including the imprisonment of Salcedo. But Gonzalo weathered the storm and remained in Nicaragua engaged in various official and commercial enterprises until his return to Panamá, in May 1529. It was during this period that he composed his *Libro del blasón* and made many of the personal observations on Central America later incorporated in his *Historia general...*

Later in that year, or possibly in 1530, he returned to Castile as «Procurador», or agent, of the municipalities of Panamá and Santo Domingo to the Spanish court. He seems to have been at Avila in 1530, and in April 1532 he was putting the finishing touches to his *Catálogo real...* at Medina del Campo. His nomination as chronicler of the Indies was made the next month and approved in August of that year with an annual salary of 30,000 maravedis. In October he secured a modification of the terms of his appointment which would permit him to request written reports from royal officials in various parts of the Indies, rather than visiting them in person as originally implied. His post of Inspector was transferred to his son Francisco González de Valdés. He returned to Santo Domingo late in 1532 to be appointed acting commander of the fortress there upon the death of the incumbent in January 1533. In October 1533 he was officially confirmed as *Alcaide*, or garrison commander, a post he was to hold without interruption until his death in 1557.

In August 1534 he disembarked at Seville with the manuscript of the First Part of the *Historia general...* which would come from the press of Juan Cromberger on September 30, 1535. In Madrid, besides seeking personal concessions and favors as always, he presented the Emperor manuscript of his *Epílogo real...* and composed the first draft of his *Libro de la cámara*... Sometime shortly after the appearance of this *Historia*... He returned Hispaniola where he now possessed estates on the Haina River and at San Juan de la Maguana, plus considerable real property in the city of Santo Domingo.

Upon arrival his immediate concern was the refitting and repair of the fortress entrusted to his care, a task which was to consume several years. He also took upon himself the role of counsellor, and from this time on the archives contain lengthy letters of information and advice on Indian matters addressed to the Council of the Indies, Prince Philip, and the Sovereigns themselves. In 1537 he received word of the death of his only surviving son, Francisco, who drowned in a river near Arequipa in November of 1536 while accompanying the expedition of Diego de Almagro on its return from Chile. The aging chronicler remained at his post, fulfilling his historial and military obligations, for ten years. In August 1546 he embarked for what, Ríos to the contrary notwithstanding, was probably his final journey to the homeland.

November of 1546 found him in Madrid, thence he followed the Council of the Indies to Aranda until the winter cold obliged this veteran of tropical service to take refuge in Seville. A second «edition» of the First Part of his *Historia general*... was printed at Salamanca by Juan de Junta in 1547, but there is no evidence that the author had any part in its preparation. Save for spelling variants and slight differences in initial letters and wood-cuts the text is substantially identical with that of the Seville edition of 1535. During this period he also prepared his final revisions of the *Libro de la cámara*..., may have also begun work on the *Batallas y quincuagenas*... which were perhaps incomplete at the time of his death. In 1548 the house of Domingo Robertis, Seville, published *Reglas de la vida espiritual y secreta teología* which our chronicler tells us was a translation from the Italian. So far as I know, no student of Oviedo has succeeded in identifying the author or the title of the «Tuscan» original, although from the similarity of titles it may have been, as pointed out below, the *Regola della vita spirituale... di frate Cherubino* first printed at Florence in 1477, In 1548 he also made the final entries in the *Historia general*... as we now know it. Ríos and others have assumed that he continued working on and adding to it for the nine years of life which still remained, and this is entirely in character. Nevertheless, no event described in the text as we know it today is later than the beginning of '49 at the very latest. So unless there is in existence a manuscript of the promised Fourth Part and / or further additions to the first three which are not described by any of the sources to which I have had access, we must consider the *Historia*..., in its present form, complete by the end of 1548. Could the original manuscript used by Ríos, which today presumably rests in the Salazar Collection of the Royal Academy of History, have been deposited in the Casa de Contratación by our Alcaide on this final visit to the peninsula?

He returned to his beloved Santo Domingo in early 1549. In 1551 he arranged a marriage for his daughter Juana with the nephew of old friend and neighbours the Bishop of San Juan, Don Rodrigo de Bastidas. In January of 1555 he forwarded a copy of the *Quincuagenas*..., perhaps his last completed literary work, to Prince Philip. Apparently he did not, as Ríos gratuitously assumed, return to Spain to oversee the printing of the Second Part of the *Historia general*... the first book of which, Book XX of the whole, came from the press of Francisco Fernández de Córdoba in 1557, nor did he live to see this which would be the last Spanish printing of any of his works for more than two hundred years. The night of 27 of June in that year he died in the fortress which the Emperor had twenty-four years earlier committed to his care, its keys still clutched in his stiffening hands.

Such, in brief chronological outline, was the career of one of the earliest and ablest observers of the New World islands and continents. Much greater and more picturesque detail and varied, often conflicting, appraisals of the value of his work can be found in the sources listed herein.

As pointed out in my opening paragraphs there does not appear to be any readily accessible, reasonably complete listing of the printed editions of Oviedo's works in their several languages. Nor has there been any extensive bibliographical study which accurately reflects his place in the history of early Spanish exploration and conquest of the Americas. He has been too often condemned or ignored by members of the two camps into which present-day American historians of this period sometimes tend to divide themselves: «Columbists» and «Casists». The partisans of Christopher Columbus follow the lead of Fernando Colón who took umbrage at certain chapters in the *Historia general*... in which an official chronicler in a legalistic age made a rather naïve attempt to prove that the title of the Spanish crown to the Indies antedated by centuries the first voyage of the great discoverer. The followers of Las Casas would carry on beyond the grave the bitter rivalry which separated these two opposing judges of the American scene in life.

The present study is designed to in some small measure fill these needs. In the first part we have tried to list every known edition, whole or partial, of Oviedo's works in their original Castilian and in other languages in which printed versions exist. In addition, we include those works know to exist in manuscript together with the location of each manuscript or manuscript in so far as this can be determined. These are listed chronologically in order of their completion, an order which, in some instances, departs considerably from that given by Ríos and other Oviedan bibliographers for reasons which will be noted under the appropriate entry.

The second part is comprised of a listing of a number of works which have drawn heavily on Oviedo's writings as source materials, which contain some critical assessment of his work, or, in a few instances, books which contribute to a better understanding of the period in which he lived and wrote. Where the title is not self-explanatory we have included a brief annotation as to the significance of the entry. These have been set down in alphabetical, rather than chronological, order since it has not always been possible to consult the original edition or to determine exact date of composition.

The reader is invited, and indeed urged, to submit corrections and additions to the bibliography offered here. My files are set up to receive criticism.

UNIVERSITY OF NORTH CAROLINA AT CHARLOTTE
December 15, 1966

PRINCIPAL BIBLIOGRAPHICAL RESOURCES CONSULTED

Antonio, Nicolás. *Biblioteca hispana vetus.* Rome, A. de Rubeis, 1696.
Arbolí y Faraudo, D. Servando, et al., ed. *Biblioteca Colombina. Catálogo de sus Libros Impresos.* Seville & Madrid, 1888-1948. [Editor and imprint vary]. 7 vols.
Beristáin de Souza, José Mariano. *Biblioteca Hispano-Americana.* Mexico, Librería Navarro, 1947-51. 8 vols.
Bibliothéque Nationale, Paris. *Catalogue Général des Livres Imprimés.*
British Museum. General Catalogue of Printed Books.
Escudero y Perosso, Francisco. *Tipografía hispalense.* Madrid, Sucesores de Rivadeneyra, 1894.
Gallardo, Bartolomé José. *Ensayo de una biblioteca española de libros raros y curiosos.* Madrid, M. Rivadeneyra, 1863-69. 4 vols.
Graesse, Jean Georges Théodore. *Trésor des Livres Rares et Précieux.* New York, S. Hacker, c. 1950. 8 vols.
Handbook of Latin American Studies. [Place & imprint vary], 1935-1963. Vols. I-XXV.
The Hispanic Society of America. Catalogue of the Library.
Library of Congress. Catalog of Printed Books.
Medina, José Toribio. *Biblioteca Hispano-Americana.* Santiago de Chile, En Casa del Autor, 1898-1907. 7 vols.
Palau y Dulcet, Antonio. *Manual del librero hispano-americano.* [A-Q]. Barcelona, Librería Palau, 1948-62. 14 vols.
Pérez Pastor, Cristóbal. *Bibliografía madrileña.* Madrid, Tip. de los huérfanos, 1891-1907. 3 vols.
—————. *La imprenta en Toledo.* Madrid, Imp. de M. Tello, 1887.
Sánchez Alonso, B. *Fuentes de la Historia Española e Hispanoamericana.* Madrid, Revista de Filología Española, 1952. 3 vols.
Simón Díaz, José. *Manual de bibliografía de la literatura española.* Barcelona, G. Gili, 1963.
Vindel, Francisco. *Manual Gráfico-Descriptivo del Bibliófilo Hispanoamericano.* Madrid, F. Vindel, 1930-34. 12 vols.

In addition to the foregoing, bibliographical works which contain a critical evaluation of our author are included under the name of their compiler in the second part of the present study.

WORKS ATTRIBUTED TO GONZALO FERNANDEZ DE OVIEDO Y VALDES

Vida del Cardenal

1. *Memorial de la vida y acciones del Cardenal D. Fr. Francisco Jiménez de Cisneros.*

Beristáin de Souza follows the lead of Nicolás Antonio and Juan Álvarez de Baena in attributing a work of this title to Oviedo. He says that it existed in ms. in the library of the Colegio Mayor at Alcalá and that it was used by Álvaro Gómez de Castro as a source for his *Historia latina del cardenal...* and by Fr. Pedro Quintanilla for his *Vida en castellano*. At mid-nineteenth century Amador de los Ríos was unable to find any trace of the manuscript and suggested that it may have been an extract from the *Batallas y Quincuagenas...* or possibly from the *Catálogo real...* Lacking any clue as to the date of composition we are listing it here as Cisneros died November 8, 1517.

Claribalte

2. *Libro del muy esforçado y inuencible Cauallero dela Fortuna propiamēte llamado don claribalte q̃ segū su verdadera interpretaciō quiere dezir don Felix o bienaventurado... nuevamente escrito y venido a noticia dela lengua castellana por medio de gonçalo Fernandez de Ouiedo alias de sobrepeña.* Valencia, Juan Viñao, 1519.

Historians of literature have made much of the fact that although the Alcaide of Santo Domingo ridicules romances of chivalry in his later writings his earliest printed work was in fact a romance of chivalry. Despite Ríos credulity, we may discard as pro-forma the author's assertion that this is a translation of a manuscript found in the «kingdom of Phirolt». On the other hand I find no reason to challenge, as does Pérez de Tudela Bueso, his claim that most of it was written «...estādo yo en la india y postrera pte accidental q̄ a presente se sabe...» which would mean in Santa María la Antigua del Darién during 1514 and 1515.

The book is dedicated to Oviedo's former patron Don Fernando de Aragon, Duke of Calabria, in the hope that it will alleviate the tedium of his imprisonment in the castle of Jativa. This dedication was not the act of political courage which it might at first seem since Fernando's release had been ordered in the testament of Ferdinand the Catholic and our chronicler probably anticipated his early return to favor. The Duke's imprisonment was to last four more years, but there is no record of his requesting a sequel to the *Claribalte* which its author had offered him.

The plot concerns the adventures of Claribalte, or Don Felix, oldest child of Duke Ponorio who is brother and heir of Emperor Grifol of Constantinople and his wife Clariosa who is the sister of Ardiano, King of Albania, at whose court they reside. The events of his career may be grouped under three general headings: the courtship of Dorendayna, Princess of England; the Albanian tournaments; and the conquest of Constantinople. The style, as Fitzmaurice-Kelly has observed, is leaden.

The «alias Sobrepeña» of the title led Hurtado and Palencia to conclude that the writer of *Claribalte* was not our chronicler but «his homonym... a citizen of Madrid». More recently Uría Ríu has established that Oviedo's father was one Miguel de Sobrepeña, hence this is a patronymic. The woodcut of the frontispiece shows a lean, bearded man kneeling to present a copy of the book to the Duke. It is assumed that this is a representation of the author.

3. *Libro del muy esforçado y inuencible cauallero de la Fortuna...* (facsimile edition of the foregoing). Madrid, Real Academia Española, 1956.

Sumario

4. *Oviedo de la natural hystoria delas Indias. Con previlegio dela S. C. C. M.* [colophon] *El p̄sente tratado intitulado Ouiedo dela natural hystoria delas Indias se imprimio a costas del autor Gõçalo Fernãdez de Ouiedo al's de Valdes. Por industria del maestre Remõ de petras y se acabo en la cibdad de Toledo a xv dias del mes de Hebrero de MDXXVȷ̃ años.*

Although it was to wait more than two hundred years for a second Spanish printing this work has proven the most durably popular of all its writer's productions. An independent work it is often known as the «Sumario» and is in fact a sort of summary of the first nineteen books, or first part, of the later *Historia general...*

5. *De la natural historia de las Indias.* [in Andrés González Barcía. *Historiadores primitivos de las Indias,* I. pp. 173 ff.] Madrid, 1749.

The second Spanish edition.

6. *De la natural historia de las Indias.* [in Enrique de Vedia. *Historiadores primitivos de Indias. (Biblioteca de Autores Españoles,* XXII. pp. 471-515)]. Madrid, Rivadaneyra, 1858.

7. *De la natural historia de las Indias. (Sumario de historia natural de las Indias). Con un estudio preliminar y notas por Enrique Álvarez López.* Madrid, Editorial Summa, 1942.

8. *Sumario de la natural historia de las Indias.* [Biblioteca Americana. Serie Cronistas de Indias.] *Edición, introducción y notas de José Miranda.* Mexico-Buenos Aires, Fondo de Cultura Económica, 1950.

9. *Sumario de la natural historia de las Indias. Ed. de Juan Bautista Avalle-Arce.* Salamanca, Ediciones Anaya, n. d. (ca. 1963).

10. *Libro secondo delle Indie occidentalie (composto da Gonzalo Ferdinando del Oviedo, altrimenti di Valde, tradotto di lingua castigliana in italiana)...* Venice, 1534.

The *Libro primo...* contains translation of Peter Martyr, the third volume of Jérez. Palau lists this series as: *Summario de la generale historia de l'Indie occidentali cavato da libri scritti del signor Pietro Martyre et da molte altre relacioni. Libri 3.*
Ana López de Meneses belives that the Venetian ambassador Andrea Navagero was the translator of Oviedo.

11. *Summario de la cose de la Indie occidentale intitulato Nova castiglia...* Rome, 1535.

Palau adds that the French translation by Jacques Gohory, printed at Paris in 1545, was made from this text.

12. *Sommario...* [in G. B. Ramusio. *Delle navigationi... Terzo volume,* pp. 44-74]. Venice, Giunti, 1556.

Ramusio was a friend and correspondent of Oviedo.

13. *Sommario...* [in G. B. Ramusio. *Delle navigationi... Terzo volvme.* pp. 44-74]. Venice, Giunti, 1565.

A reprint of the edition of 1556.

14. *Sommario...* [in G. B. Ramusio. *Delle navigationi... Terzo volume.*] Venice, Giunti, 1606.

Volume III of Ramusio's collection appears to have had fewer editions than either Volume I or Volume II. This is the third edition which contains some material not included in the first or second.

15. *L'histoire de la terre Neuve du Perù en l'Inde occidentale... nommée la Nouvelle Castille traduite de l'italien en françoys...* Paris, Pierre Gaultier..., 1545.

Palau says that this is a translation by Jacques Gohory of the Rome edition of the *Summario...* of 1535. However, the inclusion of Peru in the title suggests the presence of additional material such as Xerez's *Conquista del Perú* which was first printed in 1534, subsequently incorporated by Oviedo into the third part of his *Historia general...*

16. *The hystorie of the Weste Indies* [in Richard Eden. *The Decades of the Newe World or West India.* r^{ros} 173-214.] London, Guilhelmi. Powell, 1555.

«I have therefore thought good to ioyne to the Decades of Peter Martyr certeyne things which I have gathered out of his (Oviedo's) book intiteled the Summarie or abbrigement of his generall hystorie of the West Indies.» Folio 171r.

17. *The hystorie of the Weste Indies.* [in *The History of Trauayle in the West and East Indies.* Gathered in part and done into English by Richard Eden. F^{os} 185-225] London, Richard Iugge, 1577.

18. *Extracts of Gonzalo Ferdinando De Oviedo his Summarie and General Historie of the Indies.* [in Samuel Purchas. *Hakluytus Posthumus or Purchas his Pilgrimes.*] London, Samuel Purchas, for Henry Fetherstone, 1625.

19. *The Natural History of the West Indies, First Printed in 1526.* [in Edward Arber *The first three English Books on America,* pp. 205-242]. Birmingham, 1885.

Reprint of the Eden translation.

20. *The Natural History of the West Indies...* Westminster, 1895.

Reissue of the Arber text above.

21. *Extracts of Gonzalo Ferdinando De Oviedo his Summarie...* [Hakluyt Society, Extra Series. XV. pp. 148-232] Glasgow, James MacLehose and Sons, 1906.

Reproduces the Purchas' edition of 1625.

22. *Natural History of the West Indies by Gonzalo Fernández de Oviedo y Valdés.* Translated and Edited by Sterling A. Stoudemire. Chapel Hill, University of North Carolina Press, 1959.

An excellent modern translation of the complete text.

LABERINTO DE AMOR

23. *Laberinto de amor* (a translation of Giovanni Boccaccio's *Il corbaccio*).

Writing in the *Revista de la Biblioteca, Archivo y Museo del Ayuntamiento de Madrid* in 1935, Amada López de Meneses by her article «Gonzalo Fernández de Oviedo, traductor del Corbaccio» drew attention to a cedula of January 13, 1526 granting Oviedo permission to publish and sell a translation of this work. Pérez de Tudela cites a similar document (Archivo General Simancas, *Cédulas de la Cámara,* lib. 75, fol. 93v-94) dated January 19, 1526 and Otte one found in the *Archivos de Protocolos de Sevilla* dated May 4, 1526. The manuscript, if one existed, has been lost. The first printed Spanish translation of *Il corbaccio* appears to be the one brought out by Andrés de Burgos at Seville over twenty years later on August 3, 1546 with title as given above. This is commonly attributed to Diego López de Ayala but may be the one contemplated by our chronicler.

LIBRO PRIMERO DEL BLASON...

24. *Libro del blasón. Tratado de todas las armas é diferencias dellas, é de los escudos é diferencias que en ellos hay, é de la orden que se debe guardar en las dichas armas, para que sean ciertas no falsas, é de las colores e metales que hay en armeria, é de las reglas é circunstancias á este efeto convenientes.*

Biblioteca de la Real Academia de la Historia, Ms. 9-21-5-96, fols. 1-45. The first of a projected eleven books of a considerable treatise on heraldry. The rest of the. Ms. contains a partial copy of the *Batallas y Quincuagenas...* which is perhaps why Ríos dates it as around 1550 or 1551. However a passage quoted by Pérez de Tudela states that it was written in the city of «León de Nicaragua» which would date it ca. 1528.

Relación de... la prisión del rey de Francia

25. *Relación de lo sucedido en la prision del rey de Francia, desde que fué traido en España, por todo el tiempo que estuvo en ella, hasta que el emperador le dió libertad y volvió en Francia, casado con Madama Leonor, hermana del emperador Carlos V, rey de España. Escrita por el capitan Gonzalo Hernandez de Oviedo y Valdés, alcaide de la fortaleza de la ciudad de S. Domingo, de la Isla Española, y coronista de la Sac. Cesár. y Cathól. Maj. del Emper. Carlos V, y de la Sereniss. Reina D.ª Juana su madre.*

Biblioteca Nacional (Madrid) Ms. 8.756.156 ff. (?) [Both Ríos and Pérez de Tudela make it 165 ff.].

Inexplicably both Ríos and Pérez would have this antedate the *Sumario*, an impossibility since the principle narrative reports the birth of the future Phillip II on May 21, 1527. Both editors reject the transcript of a letter dated Rome, October 1, 1532, from Micer May, the Imperial Ambassador to Oviedo's fromer protector, the Duke of Calabria, describing the war of Naples. But I find no reason to assume that this was not added to the *Relación...* by our Alcaide. This would give us a date of 1533.

26. *Relacion de lo suscedido en la prision de el Rey de Francia desde que fue traydo en España por todo el tiempo que stuvo en ella, hasta que el Emperador le dió la libertad y bolvió en Francia casado con Madama Leonor hermana del Emperador Carlos quinto, Rey de España, por el capitan Gonzalo Fernandez de Oviedo, Natural de Madrid.* [Appendix II, Vol. II of D. José Amador de los Ríos and D. Juan de Dios de la Rada y Delgado, *Historia de la Villa y Corte de* Madrid, M. López de la Hoya, 1862 (pp. 459-470).

Apparently the first printed edition. Omits the May letter mentioned above.

27. *Relacion de lo sucedido en la prision del rey de Francia, desde que fué traido en España, por todo el tiempo que estuvo en ella, hasta que el emperador le dió libertad y volvió en Francia, casado con Madama Leonor, hermana del emperador Carlos V, rey de España.* [in *Colección de documentos inéditos para la historia de España. XXXVIII.* Madrid, Imprenta de la Vda. de Calero, 1861 (pp. 404-492).

Contains complete text of Ms. including account of the war of Naples.

WORKS ATTRIBUTED

28. *La prisión de Francisco I en Madrid...,* Madrid, Sucres de Hernando, S. A., n. d.

Edited by Modesto Pérez, this is the most recent printing.

Catálogo Real de Castilla...

29. *Catálogo Real de Castilla, y de todos los reyes de las Españas e de Nápoles y Secilia e de los reyes y señores de las Casas de Francia, Austria, Holanda y Borgoña; de donde proceden los cuatro abolorios del emperador don Carlos, nuestro señor, con relación de todos los emperadores y summos pontiices que han sucedido desde Julio César, que fué el primero emperador, y desde el apóstol Sanct Pedro, que fué el primero papa, hasta el año de Cristo MDXXXII.*

Biblioteca del Escorial, Ms. H-j-7. Autograph ms. of 451 ff.

This is probably the *Ginología de los reyes de España*, begun, according to our author at the instance of Ferdinand the Catholic ca. 1505. There is in existence a letter to Oviedo from the secretary Conchillos which acknowledges a promise to forward a copy of this genealogy as early as 1518.

30. *Epílogo Real, imperial y pontifical... Año MDXXXV*. Biblioteca Nacional (Madrid), Ms. 6.224. Also autograph, largely illegible.

Pérez believe this is the final complete draft of the *Catálogo...* cited above and that Ríos had access to the fair copy, since lost. But he disagrees with Ríos statement that the *Epílogo* seems to form the second and third parts of the *Catálogo*. Beristain de Souza dates it some twenty years earlier (i. e. 1515) with the title as *Catálogo Real...* and says that it was used by Argote de Medina as a source for his *Historia de la Nobleza de Andalucía* and that Nicolás Antonio believed it identical with a *Memorial de algunas cosas de los Reyes Católicos y del Emperador* which he found in the library of D. Gaspar Ibañez de Segovia, Marqués de Mondéjar at Madrid. More recently Enrique Otte has affirmed that this work was «terminada e impresa en 1535» a statement I am unable to confirm from any other source.

Historia General y Natural de las Indias

31. *La historia general de las Indias. Con priuelegio imperial.* [colophon: *Fin dela primera parte dela general y natural historia delas Indias islas y tierra firme del mar oceano... La* *qual se acabo y imprimio en la muy noble y muy leal cibdad de Seuilla en la imprēta de Iuan Cromberger el postrero dia del mes de Setiembre año de mil y quinientos y treynta y cinco años.*] Seville, Juan Cromberger, 1535.

The first edition of the first part of Oviedo's *magnum opus*. It contains the first nineteen books and the Prohemio, chapters 1 — 10 of the fiftieth book of this encyclopedic description of the New World. This first part is chiefly concerned with sea routes to the Indies and the Antilles. Part II, which was not to see print till mid-nineteenth century, was to describe the Atlantic coast of the mainland from the Strait of Magellan to Labrador, Part III, all that was known of the Pacific coast.

32. *Cronica delas Indias. La hystoria de las Indias agora nueuamente impressa corregida y emendada. 1547.* Salamanca, Juan de Junta, 1547. Often found bound with Francisco de Xerez's *Conquista del Perú* issued by the same press approximately two months later. (First printed in 1534). Oviedo was to incorporate Xerez's account in his own Part III. There has been some question as to whether our historian personally supervised the printing of this second edition of the first part of his *Historia general...* although he is known to have been in Spain at time. There does not seem to be any published analysis of differences between the first and second editions which are substantially identical save for spelling variants.

33. *Libro XX. Dela segunda parte dela general historia delas Indias. Escripta por el Capitan Gonzalo Fernandez de Ouiedo y Valdes, Alcayde de la fortaleza y puerto de Sācto Domingo, d'la isla Española, Cronista de su Magestad. Que trata del estrecho de Magallanes.* Valladolid, Francisco Fernández de Córdoba, 1557.

At the end of Chapter xxxv is the statement «No se imprimio mas desta obra, por que murio el autor.» which has led Ríos and others to erroneously assume that Oviedo died in Valladolid. Agapito Rey has postulated an earlier edition, possibly coetaneous with the Salamanca printing of the First part in 1547. Juan M. Sánchez in his *Impresores y libros impresos en Aragón en el siglo XVI...* (Madrid, Impr. Alemana, 1938) mentions a *Historia de Indias* by one Gonzalo Oviedo printed at Zaragoza in 1554, but he does not give the name of printer and I am unable to confirm his reference from any other source.

Because of the date of printing of this first book of the second part both Ríos and Pérez de Tudela list the *Historia general...* last in their *orden cronológico*. However there is no evidence that anything was added to the text as we now know it after 1548.

34. [*Historia general...* the 'Monserrate Ms.']

Pérez de Tudela asserts that the original autograph manuscripts by Oviedo of his 'Additions' to the first part, and of the rest of his *Historia general...*, save for Book XXVIII, are found in the Muñoz and Salazar collections of the library of the Royal Academy of History. Presumably, the autograph originals are in the Colección Salazar since 1) Alvarez de Baena informs us that the original were initially deposited in the Casa de Contratación and afterwards came into to possession of Don Luis de Salazar who bequeathed them with the rest of his library to the Royal Monastery of Monserrate de Madrid, and 2) the detailed *Catálogo de la colección J. Bautista Muñoz* published by the Academy in 1954 lists only eighteenth century copies of various parts of the *Historia general...* in this collection. Muñoz had access to the «manuscrito de Monserrate» and used it as a basis for his definitive text, later utilized by Ríos.

35. [*Historia general... Libro XXVIII*].

Ms. copy in «los fondos de jesuitas» of the Royal Academy of History, Madrid. Both Ríos and Pérez de Tudela attest to the presence in this copy of a book not found elsewhere. Jiménez de la Espada indicates Tomo 108, *Varios papeles de jesuitas,* al fol. 309.

36. [*Historia general... 2da Pte.*].

Ms. in the *Biblioteca Colombina.* It appears that the *copia(s) de diversos libros* which Pérez de Tudela attributes to the *Biblioteca colombina* of Seville must be the copy of Books XX- XXXVIII (less XXVIII?), i. e. the second part, of an «ancient copy» made from what we today call the Monserrate manuscript and described by Alvarez de Baena.

37. [*Adiciones a la Primera parte de la Historia*].

Col. Muñoz, *Tomo 7, Nos.* 36, 37, 38. For a detailed description see pp. 36, Vol. I of the Real Academia de la Historia's *Catálogo de la colección J. Bautista Muñoz,* Madrid, Imprenta y Editorial Maestre, 1954. The intriguing thing is that while Amador de los Ríos mentions the Muñoz manuscripts, the catalogue seems to indicate that the printed version of Ríos and his successors differs considerably from the present Ms. at least in the number of Chapters; to wit: Muñoz adds 7 chapters to the 8 in Ríos' version of Book X; to Book XIII he adds 5; to Book XIV, 23; to Book XV, 13; to Book XVII, 2; to Book XIX, 1 the foregoing according to Muñoz' *'indice'.*

38. [*Historia general... Libros XXIX - XXXII.*]

Col. Muñoz, *Tomo 8.* No. 39. For detailed description see *Catálogo...* cited above. Late eighteenth century hand.

39. [*Historia general... Libros XXXIII - XXXVII*].

Col. Muñoz, *Tomo 9,* No. 40. Late eighteenth century.
Cf. *Catálogo...* I, pp. 39-40.

40. [*Volumen segundo de la segunda parte de la Historia...*].

Col. Muñoz, *Tomo 39, No. 327* to 375 (Remaining folios contain various documents pertaining to Hernán Cortés. This is a certified true copy of Books IX — 10 through XXXII — 13 taken from Ms. in the Cathedral of Seville (*Biblioteca colombina*) and dated May 6, 1780. Cf. *Catálogo...* I, pp. 216-217.

41. [*Volumen segundo de la segunda parte de la Historia...*].

Col. Muñoz, *Tomo 40*, No. 333.
A continuation of the previous entry containing Books XXXIII-14 through XXXVIII-19. Cf. *Catálogo...* I, p. 221.

42. ...*Historia de las Indias*.

Biblioteca de Palacio, Madrid. Nos. 3040-3041.
For detailed description see: Jesús Domínguez Bordona. *Manuscritos de América. Catálogo de la Biblioteca de Palacio. IX.* Madrid, Talleres Blass, S. A., 1935, p. 2. The first 149 folios are from the printed Salamanca edition of 1547, up through Chapter 21, Book XVII. According to a note at the bottom of fol. 149 the copy of the remaining books of Part I and Parts II and III which follows is based on the author's original ms. A memorandum by Jiménez de la Espada preserved in the first volume advises that the missing chapters of Book XXVII and all of Book XXVIII are to be found in the library of the Royal Academy of History, *Varios papeles de Jesuitas*, Tomo 108, beginning at folio 309. This copy was formerly in the library of the Count of Torrepalma.

43. [...*Historia de las Indias*] 1ra & 2da *ptes.*

Ms. in he U. S. Library of Congress, Washington, D. C.
A copy of the second and third parts of Oviedo's *Historia...* from the collection of Col. Peter Force, who also owned the 1547 edition of the first part now in the same library. Mentioned by Robertson and in the *Handbook of Manuscripts in the Library of Congress*, Washington, D. C., Government Printing Office, 1918.

44. [*Historia de Indias*].

Ms. in Lenox Branch, New York Public Library, New York, N. Y.
Robertson mentions this as part of the Rich Collection without further bibliographical details.

45. [*Historia general y natural... Libros IV, VI, VII, IX, XI, XXXII* and *XXXVII*].

Mss. in the Henry E. Huntington Library, San Marino, Cal.
Cited as autograph mss by Ronald Hilton in his *Handbook of Hispanic Source Materials and Research Organizations in the United States.* Stanford, Cal., Stanford University Press, 1956.

46. *Historia general y natural de las Indias, islas y tierra firme del mar Oceano, por el capitán Gonzalo Fernández de Oviedo y Valdés, primer cronista del Nuevo Mundo. Publícala la Real Academia de la Historia cotejada con el códice original, enriquecida con las enmiendas y adiciones del autor, é ilustrada con la vida y juicio de las obras del mismo por d. José Amador de los Ríos...* Madrid, Imp. de la Real Academia de la Historia, 1851-55. IV vols.

The first printed edition of all three parts, based chiefly, as Ríos tells us in his Advertencia (I, pp. vi-ix) on the 1535 edition and what we have described above as the 'Monserrate manuscript'. As Peña y Cámara has pointed out, this is hardly in any sense a 'critical edition' for the editor has failed to indicate clearly the author's additions and changes to the first part. I might add that he has, by his own admission, 'regularized' the spelling, and altered the system of annotation. Subsequent research has also raised question as to the accuracy of Ríos' highly praised preliminary essay on the «Vida y escritos de Gonzalo Fernández de Oviedo y Valdés.» Peña has termed the biographical portion a «novelita rosa,» while the bibliographical portion is unsatisfactory in matters of chronology and bibliographical detail.

47. *Historia general y natural de las Indias, Islas y Tierra-Firme del Mar Océano. Prólogo de J. Natalicio González; notas de José Amador de los Ríos.* Asunción del Paraguay, Editorial Guaranía, 1944-45. 14 vols.

The *Prólogo* summarizes without documentation the biographical and bibliographical data supplied by Ríos and the text follows that of his Academy edition of Madrid, 1851-55.

48. *Historia general y natural de las Indias. Edición y estudio preliminar (Vida y escritos de G. Fernández de Oviedo) de J. Pérez de Tudela.* Madrid, Real Academia Española, 1959. 5 vols. [*Biblioteca de Autores Españoles*, CXVII-CXXI].

The *Estudio preliminar* supersedes Ríos treatment of Oviedo's life and works, provides an invaluable synthesis of research in these areas up to date of publication. Another valuable addition is the geograpihc and onomastic index, comprising some six thousand entries, at the end of volume V. The text, unfortunately, save for certain modernization of orthography is that of the edition of 1851-55.

Extracts or selections from the «Historia General...»

49. Lib. XLVII, cap. 1 - 67 [in *Colección de historiadores de Chile...*, Santiago de Chile, 1901. Vol. XXII, pp. 1 -254].

50. *Selecciones de la Historia general...* [in José Toribio Medina, *Colección de historia de Chile*, Santiago de Chile, 1901-1902. Vols. XXVII, XXIX].

51. *Historia de Indias (selecciones)*. Madrid, Bueno del Amo, 1927.

Palau lists the press as Bruno del Amo.

52. «Almagro: episodios de su vida.» *Boletín de la Academia chilena de la historia*. [Santiago de Chile] 1ro & 2do semestre, 1936, pp. 25-78.

53. O'Gorman, Edmundo, ed., *Suceso y diálogo de la Nueva España*. Mexico, Universidad Nacional Autónoma de México, 1946.

54. *Delle general et naturale historia delle Indie a tempi nostri ritrovate...* [in G. B. Ramusio, *Navigationi et viaggi*, Venice, Giunti, 1556, Vol. III].

This same volume also includes an Italian version of the *Sumario*. Oviedo boasted that the first part of his *Historia general...* had been translated into Latin, Greek, Arabic, French, German, Italian and Turkish. (*v.* p. 264, Vol. IV of the Madrid, 1959, edition cited above.). Of these alleged translations, so far as I have been able to determine, only the French and Italian have found their way into print. The *Library of Congress Catalogue* follows Ríos in stating that Latin translations of the chapters of *guayacán* and *palo santo* found their way into various collections of *Scriptores de morbo gallico*, not further identified. But Oviedo's name does not appear in the title to any of the more important of such works listed by the catalogues of the Library of the Surgeon General's Office. Peter Martyr had also spoken of the medicinal properties of these woods in his *Decades...* and in 1519, seven years before the appearance of Oviedo's *Sumario*, Ulrich von Hutten had published at Strassburg his *Von der wunderbarlichĕ artzney des holtz Guaiacum genant, und wie man die Frantzosen oder blatteren heilen sol... Durch... T. Murner... geteutschet*. There may be some connection between the *Sumario* and Girolamo Fracastoro's *Syphilis sive morbus gallicus*, the first edition of which appeared at Verona in 1530, since our chronicler mentions this author in his *Historia general...*, but the first edition Fracastoro's Latin poem anticipates the *Historia* by some five years.

55. *Delle general et naturale historia delle Indie. a tempi nostri ritrovate...* [in G. B. Ramusio, *Navigationi et viaggi, III*] Venice, Giunti, 1565.

Second printing of above.

56. *Delle general et natvrale historia delle Indie a tempi nostri ritrovate...* [in G. B. Ramusio, *Navigationi et viaggi, III*] Venice, Giunti, 1606.

Third printing, but really second and enlarged edition of this volume. Somewhere I have seen reference to a fourth printing, Venice, in 1746. I am unable to confirm this last edition.

57. *L'Histoire Natvrelle e generalle des Indes, isles et Terre Ferme de la grand Mer Oceane...* Paris, Michel de Vascosan, 1555.

Reportedly identical with the edition from the same press in the following year, save that this latter includes the name of the translator, Jean Poleur, on the title page. Both Medina and Sabin say this is a translation of the first TEN books of the *Historia general...*, according to Palau only the first SIX.

58. *L'Histoire Natvrelle e generalle des Indes, isles et Terre Ferme de la grand Mer Oceane... Traduicte de castillan en françois par Jean Poleur...* Paris, Michel de Vascosan, 1556.

See note on 1555 edition above.

59. *Histoire du Nicaragua par Gonzalo Fernandez de Oviedo y Valdes...* [in H. Ternaux-Compans, *Voyages, relations et mémoires originaux pour servir à l'histoire de la découverte de L'Amerique...XIV*] Paris, A. Bertrand, 1840.

Translation of Chapters 1 — 13, Book XLII of the *Historia general...*

60. *...an account based on the diary of Rodrigo Ranjel... tr. from the Spanish...* [in E. G. Bourne, *Narratives of the Career of Hernando de Soto...*] New York, Allerton Book Company, 1922.

61. «Selections from Oviedo's *Historia de Indias* [Appendix to Fr. Gaspar de Carvajal, *The Discovery of the Amazon...*] New York, American Geographic Society, 1934.

Libro de la Cámara

62. *Libro de la camara real del principe don Juan e officios de su casa e seruicio ordinario, compuesto por Gonçalo Fernandez de Ouiedo...*

Llacayo y Santa María in his *Antiguos manuscritos... del Escorial*, Seville, Francisco Alvarez y C^{ia}, 1878 [*Sociedad de Bibliófilos Andaluces*, 2da ser., X. p. 149] tells us that the autograph ms. is in the Escorial. Both Ríos and Pérez de Tudela mention the existence of numerous ms. copies. The former writes of five copies, with varying titles, in the Biblioteca Nacional alone, the latter, copies in the Biblioteca Nacional, Biblioteca de Palacio, Real Academia de la Historia, and cites Miguélez to the effect that the autograph rests in the Biblioteca del Escorial.

An interesting account of the organization and ceremonial of the household of the only son of Ferdinand and Isabel, in which our chronicler served as *el mozo que tenia las llaves de la cámara* (a sort of supply sergeant or book-keeper), It was written for the use of the future Phillip II.

63. *Libro de la camara real del principe don Juan...* Madrid, Imp. de la viuda é hijos de Galiano, 1870. [edited by D. José María de la Peña, *Sociedad de Bibliófilos Españoles. VII*].

First and only printed edition.

Regla de la Vida Espiritual

64. *Regla de la Vida espiritual y Teología secreta.* Seville, Domingo Robertis, 1548.

In *Las Quincuagenas...* Oviedo tells us this was a translation from the Italian and that it enjoyed a very poor sale. Succeeding bibliographers are equally vague as to the identity of the original. From the similarity of titles I suspect that it may be a version of the *Regola della vita spirituale... di frate Cherubino*, printed at Florence in 1477 and again in 1487. There is at least one reference to Fr. Cherubino in the *Quincuagenas*.

Libro de Linajes

65. *Libro de linajes y armas que escribió el capitán Gonzalo Fernández de Oviedo y Valdés, coronista del emperador Carlos V y de las Indias.*

Ms. in Colección Salazar of the Real Academia de la Historia, C. 24. Ríos assigned this *nobiliario* a date of 1552. Pérez de Tudela says that date is unknown but that content is similar to that of some of the *Batallas*... He says that the ms. is eighteenth century. Miralles de Imperial citing, under slightly different title, what appears to be the same ms., identifies it as a xvi century copy.

LAS QUINCUAGENAS

66. *Las Quincuagenas de los generosos e illustres e no menos famosos reyes, príncipes, duques, marqueses, y condes e caballeros e personas notables de España, que escribió el capitán Gonzalo Fernández de Oviedo y Valdés, alcaide de Sus Majestades en la fortaleza de la cibdad e puerto de Sancto Domingo de la Isla Española, coronista de las Indias, isla e Tierra Firme del mar Océano, vecino y regidor desta cibdad e natural de la muy noble e leal villa de Madrid.*

Biblioteca Nacional, Mss. 2.217 - 2.218 - 2.219. 3 vols. fol. mayor.

The letter of transmittal, addressed to Prince Phillip is dated January 1555.

Quincuagena... as defined by the author for the purposes of this text is a poem of fifty stanzas of fifty verses each. The present work is built on a framework of three quincuagenas or 7500 verses which Oviedo calls «segunda rima», i. e. verses of seven or eight syllables, couplets, in consonantal rhyme rather than the assonance which is characteristic of Spanish ballad structure. On the basis of these Menéndez Pelayo has termed Oviedo the first Spanish-American poet, while admitting that they are devoid of poetic or literary merit. The great bulk of the text, however, consists of glosses or commentaries on the commonplaces and pious platitudes expressed in rhyme. These are of interest because of the light they shed on historic persons and events. Because of similarity of title, this is often confused with the unfinished *Batallas y quincuagenas...* in dialog form.

67. *Las quincuagenas de los generosos y no menos famosos Reyes, Príncipes, Duques... Ed. D. Vicente de la Fuente.* I (único publicado). Madrid, Imprenta y Fundición de Manuel Tello, 1880.

Only one volume (i. e. the first *quincuagena,* the first third) has been printed. Morel-Fatio in a well known review (in *Revue Historique* XXI, p. 197 ff) has criticized the editor for apparent carelessness in transcription and questions the choice of this ms. for publication rather than the more interesting *Batallas y quincuagenas*.

Respuesta a la Epístola moral del Almirante

68. *Esta es una muy notable y moral Epístola que el muy ilustre señor Almirante de Castilla envió al autor de las sobredichas Quincuagenas, hablando de los males de España y de la causa dellos con la Respuesta del mismo autor.*

Biblioteca Nacional, Ms. 7.075. The full title differs slightly in Ríos. Pérez de Tudela in a note to his *Vida y escritos...* (*Historia general...* I, xcviii, n. 297) states that the first 17 folios of the ms. contain the «epístola» of Don Fadrique Enriquez in 12 chapters, but in his bibliography he says that Oviedo's *respuesta* occupies fols. 13-44.

Both editors date the original ca. 1524, judge this a copy in a late xvi century hand. The title suggests that it was written after the *Quincuagenas...* (January 1555) and also that the chroncler, if not the admiral, may have been influenced by Fr. Luis de Escobar's highly popular *Las quatrociētas Respuestas a otras tātas preguntas que el yllustrissimo señor dō Fradrique enrriquez: Almirante d' Castilla y otras personas... enbiarō a preguntar al autor...* first printed at Valladolid in 1545 by the same Francisco de Córdoba who was to *publish Libro XX* of Oviedo's *Historia general* twelve years later The same press produced a second edition of Escobar's work in 1550, brought out a *Segunda Parte* in 1552.

Some bibliographers erroneously say that the *Respuesta...* has been published in the *Colección de documentos inéditos para la historia de España.*

Batallas y Quincuagenas

69. *Batallas y Quincuagenas, escriptas por el capitán Gonzalo Fernández de Oviedo, criado del príncipe don Juan, etc.*

Mss. in the Biblioteca Nacional, Real Academia de la Historia and Biblioteca de Palacio are cited by Pérez de Tudela without further identifying data. He also mentions a ms. compilado by Amador de los Ríos (presumably also in the library of the Academia) which contains dialogues not included in any of the foregoing and of which he promises an edition in the near future.

Ríos dates this 1550, but in an article published posthumously in *Boletín de la Real Academia de la Historia* (I, pp. 209-217) December 1877, he confessed that he had been able to assemble no more than 338 dialogues out of a projected 600. The answer may well be that in spite of having written «cuatro gruesos volúmenes» Oviedo had not finished this great biographical compendium at the time of his death in 1557. This was used by Prescott as one of his sources for *Ferdinand and Isabella* and is undoubtedly the most frequently cited of Oviedo's unpublished works.

WORKS CITING OR CONTRIBUTING TO AN UNDERSTANDING OF OVIEDO AND HIS CONTEMPORARIES

70. [Real] Academia Española. *Diccionario de la lengua castellana en que se explica el verdadero sentido de las voces...* Madrid Francisco del Hierro, 1726-35. 5 vol.

The name of Gonzalo Fernández de Oviedo appears among the «[Autores de Prosa] Desde 1500 a 1600» in the «Lista de autores elegidos por la Real Academia Española para el uso de las voces y modos de hablar que han de explicarse en el Diccionario de la Lengua Castellana repartidos en diferentes clases, según los tiempos en que escribieron...». He is cited for his «obras» without further specification.

71. Aglio, Augustine. *Antiquities of Mexico...* (Ed. by Edward King, Lord Kingsborough). London, R. Harwell, 1830-1848. 9 vols.

The *Catalogue* of the British Museum states that Vol. 8 contains printed version on an Oviedo Ms., not further identified.

72. Alegría, Ricardo E. «Origin and Diffusion of the Term 'Cacique'». in *Selected Papers of the XXIX International Congress of Americanists. Part II.* (Ed. by Sol Tax). Chicago, University of Chicago Press, 1952, pp. 313-315.

Oviedo is cited on p. 313.

73. Alonso del Real, C. «Fernández de Oviedo y las Amazonas». *Cuadernos Hispano-Americanos.* XLII. 1961. Pp. 33-44.

74. Altamira y Crevea, Rafael. *Historia de España y la Civilización Española...* 3.ª ed. corregida y aumentada. Barcelona, Herederos de Juan Gili, 1913-1914. 4 vols.

The 1851-55 edition of Oviedo's *Historia general...* appears in the bibliography.

75. Alvarez de Baena, Joseph Antonio. *Hijos de Madrid...* Madrid, Benito Cano, 1790. 2 vols.

Biographical and bibliographical sketch of Oviedo on pp. 354-361 of Vol. II. Interesting data on custody of the original manuscript of the *Historia general*...

Alvarez López, Enrique, ed. v. Fernández de Oviedo y Valdés, G. *Natural Historia de las Indias*, Madrid..., 1942.

76. Alvarez López, Enrique. «Acerca de la obra de Fernández de Oviedo». *Boletín de la Real Sociedad Española de Historia Natural*. LVI. (1958). Pp. 39-71.

77. Alvarez López, Enrique. «Apuntes acerca de los mamíferos americanos conocidos por Fernández de Oviedo». *Associaçao Portuguesa para o Progresso das Ciências. Tomo V. 4.ª Secção, Ciências Naturais, Congresso de Porto, 1942.* Porto, Impressa Portuguesa, 1943. Pp. 445-51.

Through an editorial error this article was incorrectly attributed to «Enrique López Fernández.»

78. Alvarez López, Enrique. «La historia natural en Fernández de Oviedo». *Revista de Indias. XVII.* (69-70) Jul-Dic. 1957. Pp. 541-604.

78. Alvarez López. Enrique. «El 'perro mudo' americano». *Boletín de la Real Sociedad Española de Historia Natural. XL.* (1942). Pp. 411-417.

79. Alvarez López, Enrique. «Las plantas americanas en la botánica europea del siglo xvi». *Revista de Indias. VI.* (Abr-Jun 1943). Pp. 221-288.

80. Alvarez López, Enrique. «Plinio y Fernández de Oviedo». *Anales de Ciencias Naturales del Instituto J. de Acosta. I.* Madrid, 1940. I. Pp. 40-61; II. Pp. 13-35.

81. Alvarez López, Enrique. «La zoología en Fernández de Oviedo». *Revista de Educación. La Plata. II.* 1958. Pp. 495-509.

82. Alvarez Rubiano, Pablo. *Pedrarias Dávila. Contribución al estudio de la figura del «Gran Justiciador», Gobernador de Castilla de Oro y Nicagua.* Madrid, Consejo Superior de Investigaciones Científicas, 1944.

A doctoral thesis dealing with our chronicler's arch-enemy and superior during his early years in the New World.

83. Altolaguirre y Duvale, Angel de. *Vasco Nuñez de Balboa.* Madrid, Imp. Patronato de Huérfanos de Intendencia é Intervención Militares, 1914.

Valuable to an understanding of Oviedo's experiences in Darien. Note Document 79 (pp. 209-217), reproduction of an undated «Memorial de Gonzalo Fernández de Oviedo denunciando abusos de Pedrarias Dávila y sus Oficiales en la Gobernación de Castilla de Oro.»

Amador de los Ríos, José, *ed.*   v. Gonzalo Fernández de Oviedo, *Historia general y natural de las Indias...* Madrid, 1851-55.

84. Amador de los Ríos, José. «Sobre la publicación de las *Batallas y Quincuagenas* del capitán Gonzalo Fernández de Oviedo». *Boletín de la Real Academia de la Historia.* I. (3: Feb. 1879). Pp. 209-217.

Posthumous publication of the *Informe* presented by Ríos to the Academy on December 14, 1877 on results of his twenty-two years of investigation of the *Batallas...* As pointed out above, he had succeeded in assembling little more than half of a projected 600 dialogs.

85. Amador de los Ríos, José and Juan de Dios de la Rada y Delgado. *Historia de la Villa y Corte de Madrid.* II (of 4 vols.). Madrid, M. López de la Hoya, 1862.

Numerous citations of Oviedo, especially from the *Quincuagenas* and the *Historia general...* Oviedo's *Relación de lo suscedido en la prisión del rey de Francia...* is included as Appendix II (pp. 459-470).

86. *The American Heritage Book of Indians.* New York, Simon and Schuster, c. 1961.

On pp. 80 and 99 editors reproduce pictures from the mss. of Oviedo's *Historia general...* in the Huntington Library.

87. Andagoya, Pascual de. *Relación de los sucesos de Pedrarias Dávila en las provincias de Tierra-Firme, Castilla del Oro...* [consulted in Martín Fernández de Navarrete. *Colección de los viajes y descubrimientos... III.* Buenos Aires, Editorial Guaranía, 1945. Pp. 387-443].

Andagoya was a contemporary and acquaintance of Oviedo.

88. Anderson, C. L. G. *Old Panamá and Castilla del Oro.* New York, North River Press, 1944. (Previous editions 1911, 1938).

History in English, based chiefly on published Spanish sources. The index indicates at least twenty-two references to Oviedo.

89. Anderson-Imbert, Enrique. *Historia de la literatura hispano americana.* México-Buenos Aires, Fondo de Cultura Económica, 1954.

Cf. pp. 19-20. An evaluation of Oviedo as a historian and a philosopher «Renacentista, pero del Renacimiento español, católico, conservador de las tradiciones medievales...».

90. Anderson-Imbert, Enrique. «Raconteurs of the Conquest». *Américas.* III. Washington, D. C., Pan American Union, Oct. 1951. Pp. 7-9; 42-43.

91. Anghiera, Pietro Martire d'. *De orbe novo...* Alcalá de Henares, Miguel de Eguía, 1530.

Wagner feels that Oviedo knew only the first four decades, but I think it likely that he owned all eight in the edition cited. Anghiera, or Peter Martyr as he is known to English historians wrote in Latin. Although there were numerous translations into other European languages, the earliest printed Spanish translation seems to have been that of Madrid, 1892. I have consulted that of Joaquín Torres Asensi, *Decadas del Nuevo Mundo,* Buenos Aires, Ed. Bajel, 1944. On p. 299 of this edition is Anghiera's account of a visit paid by Oviedo to his home which must have occurred some time between the latter's return from Darien in the fall of 1515 and the publication of the Third Decade (Alcalá, November 1516). So far as I have been able to determine Oviedo nowhere mentions this encounter nor his personal acquaintance with Peter Martyr, though in the *Historia general...* he criticizes his accuracy as an historian.

92. Antelo Iglesias, Antonio. «En el centenario de la muerte de Gonzalo Fernández de Oviedo.» *Studium* (Bogotá). I. 1957. Pp. 281-289.

93. Arciniegas, Germán. *Caribbean: Sea of the New World.* (trans. by Harriet de Onís). New York, Alfred A. Knopf, 1946.

Citations from Oviedo on pp. 25, 47, 50, 54, 57, 77-78, 99, 102, 105, 107, 120, 126, 128.

94. Arciniegas, Germán. *Germans in the Conquest of America.* (trans. by Angel Flores). New York, Macmillan, 1943.

Oviedo cited in chapter vii, x, and xii.

95. Argensola, Bartolomé Leonardo de. *Primera parte de los anales de Aragón.* Zaragoza, Juan de Lanaja, 1630.

96. Argote de Molina, Gonzalo. *Nobleza del* [sic] *Andaluzia...* Sevilla, Fernando Díaz, 1558.

According to Beristáin de Souza Argote utilizó Oviedo's *Catálogo Real...* as one of his sources.

97. Armstrong, Edward. *The Emperor Charles V.* London, Macmillan, 1901. (2^d ed. 1912), 2 vols.

98. Arrate, José Martín Félix de. *Llave del Nuevo Mundo.* México, Fondo de Cultura Económica, 1949. (1st ed. La Habana, 1830).

Bibliography includes the *Sumario* and both 1535 and 1547 editions of the *Historia general...*

99. Asensio, Eugenio. «La carta de Gonzalo Fernández de Oviedo al cardenal Bembo sobre la navegación del Amazonas.» (con fasc.). *Revista de Indias,* IX. Madrid, 1949. Pp. 569-577.

Also published in *Boletín Academia Nacional de Historia, 31.* Quito, 1951. Pp. 78-86.

100. Balaguer, Joaquín. *Historia de la literatura dominicana.* Ciudad Trujillo, R. D., 1958. Pp. 26-29.

Includes an inaccurate biographical sketch, Fitzmaurice-Kelly's criticism of Oviedo's leaden style, an severe criticism of Oviedo's «insensitivity» to the beauties of the American landscape.

101. Ballesteros, M. ed. *Escritores de Indias*. Madrid, Editorial Ebro, 1941. 2 vols.

Valbuena Prat mentions selections from Oviedo, not further identified.

102. Ballesteros Beretta, Antonio. *Cristóbal Colón y el descubrimiento de América*. Barcelona, Salvat, 1945. 2 vols. [part of *Historia de América*].

See Vol. I, pp. 29-34 for an evaluation of Oviedo as a source of Columbian history.

103. Ballesteros Beretta, Antonio. *Historia de España y su influencia en la historia universal...* 2da ed. corregida y revisada por D. Manuel Ballesteros Gaibrois. Barcelona, Salvat, 1943-56. (1st ed. 1943). 10 vols.

References to Oviedo are found in vols. V, VI and VII.

104. Ballesteros Gaibrois, Manuel. «Fernández de Oviedo, etnólogo.» Revista de Indias. XVII. Madrid (Jul-Dec. 1957). Pp. 445-468.

105. Ballesteros Gaibrois, M. «Gonzalo Fernández de Oviedo: escritor e historiador». in *Libro jubilar de Emeterio S. Santovenia en su cincuentenario de Escritor*. La Habana, [imprint not given], 1957 (1958).

106. Ballesteros Gaibrois, Manuel. *Vida del madrileño Gonzalo Fernández de Oviedo y Valdés*. Madrid, Instituto de Estudios Madrileños, 1958.

107. Bancroft, Hubert Howe. *History of Central America*. San Francisco. The History Company, 1886. 2 vols. [Vols. VI & VII *The Works of H. H. B.*

Vol. I, p. 311: «Oviedo was not a learned man like Peter Martyr, and it is doubtful if a further insight into books of the day would have made him any wiser; yet a man who could dictate the natural history of a new country without his notes cannot be called illiterate.» Also see Vol. II, pp. 310-312 for critical judgement of Oviedo as an historian.

108. Bancroft, Hubert Howe. *History of Mexico*. San Francisco, The History Company, 1886. 2 vols. [Vols. IX & X of *The Works of. H. H. B.*]

Cites original edition of the *Sumario*, Ríos' edition of the *Historia general...*, and Ramusio's translations.

109. Barros Arana, Diego. *Obras completas*. Santiago de Chile, Imprenta Cervantes, 1908-14. 16 vols.

Cf. Vol. VIII, pp. 3-11, for sketch of Oviedo cited by Moses.

110. Bataillon, Marcel. «Las Casas et le licencié Cerrato». *Bulletin Hispanique*. LV (1953). Pp. 79-87.

111. Bataillon, Marcel. «Cheminement d'une légende: les 'caballeros pardos' de Las Casas». *Symposium* (Syracuse) VI (1): Pp. 1-21.

A Spanish translation of this article was to appear the following year in *La Torre*. It charges Oviedo with a deliberately distorted accout of Las Casas' plans for colonization.

112. Bataillon, Marcel. *Erasmo y España*. Mexico, Fondo de Cultura Económica, 1950. 2 vols.

Cf. Vol. I, pp. 429ff for a discussion of Erasmian ideas of Oviedo.

113. Bataillon, Marcel. «Etapas de una leyenda: los 'Caballeros Pardos' de Las Casas.» *La Torre* (Universidad de Puerto Rico) I (Oct.-Dec 1953). Pp. 41-63.

Oviedo distorted the idea of the «Caballeros Pardos» according to Bataillon.

114. Bataillon, Marcel and Edmundo O'Gorman. *Dos concepciones de la tarea histórica con motivo de la idea del descubrimiento de América. Marcel Bataillon y Edmundo O'Gorman*. Mexico, [imprint not given], 1955.

115. Bayerri Bertomeu, Enrique. *Colón tal cual fué*. Barcelona, Porter. 1961.

References to Oviedo on pp. 123, 136, 233, 382, 464, 622, 735.

116. Benzoni, Girolamo. *La Historia del mondo nuovo... La qual tratta dell' isole e mari nuovamente ritrovate, & delle nuove città da lui propio vedute, per acqua & per terre in quattordeci anni*. Venice... Rampazetto, 1565.

An Italian adventurer who was in the Americas from 1522 to 1556, Benzoni drew freely on Italian translations of Oviedo and Peter Martyr in describing events prior to his own stay in the New World. A Latin translation of Benzoni's work by Urbano Chauveton was published at Geneva in 1578, later incorporated into the *Americae pars quarta, quinta, sexta* of Theodore de Bry, Frankfurt, 1594-96 and the English, French, German and Dutch translations, of this latter work. This is probably the source of the erroneus attribution to Chauveton of a Latin translation of Oviedo.

117. Bernaldez, Andrès. *Historia de los Reyes Católicos...* Seville, Imprenta que fue de J. M. Geofrin, 1870. 2 vols. [*Bibliófilos Andaluces*. 1ra ser I & II]. (First printed edition: Granada, Imp. y Lib. de D. José María Zamora, 1856; Another, Seville, pp. 567-773, vol. III, *Crónicas de los Reyes de Castilla* [*Biblioteca de Autores Españoles* LXX], Madrid, Rivadeneyra, 1878; an *Antología...* was printed by FE, Madrid, 1945; And Aguilar has offered two editions of *Selecciones* in the *Colección Crisol,* Madrid 1946 and 1959; I am unable to verify reference to an edition printed at Seville in 1951.)

In his *Quincuagenas* the Alcaide of Santo Domingo makes frequent reference to Bernáldez, whom he calls «El cura de los Palacios.» He must have owned the *Historia de los reyes católicos...* in ms. since the earliest printed edition appears to be that of Granada cited above.

118. Blacker, Irwin R. and Harry M. Rosen. *The Golden Conquistadors...* Indianapolis, Bobbs-Merrill, 1960.

Contains a translation of the Rangel diary of the De Soto expedition taken from Oviedo's *Historia general...*

119. Blanco-Fombona, Rufino. *El conquistador español del siglo xvi.* Caracas-Madrid, Ediciones Edime, 1956.

Although Blanco-Fombona does not cite Oviedo by name, he provides a powerful evocation of the epoch in whch he lived.

120. Bourne, Edward Gaylord (trans.). «A Narrative of De Soto's Expedition Based on the Diary of Rodrigo Rangel». [in *Narratives of De Soto,* New York, Allerton Book Co., 1922. Pp. 41-158.]

121. Bourne, Edward Gaylord. *Spain in America 1450-1580.* [Vol. III, *The American Nation: A History*]. New York, Harper & Brothers, c. 1904.

Draws on Oviedo as a source. «His wide acquaintance and extensive experience in the New World were supplemented by moderation of judgement.» (p. 328).

122. Braden, Charles S. *Religious aspects of the Conquest of Mexico.* Durham, N. C., Duke University Press, 1930.

See p. 315 for an evaluation of our chronicler as a source for «historical and geographical study.»

123. Brandi, Karl. *Kaiser Karl V...* Munich, F. Bruckman, 1937. (subsequent editions: 1938, 1940, 1942).

Study of the emperor to whose service Oviedo devoted nearly half of his long career.

124. Brehm, Reinhold Bernhard. *Das Inka-reich. Beiträge zur staats- undsistten-geschichte des kaisertums Tahuantisuyu. Nach den ältesten spanischen quellen bearbeitet von dr. med. Reinhold Bernhard Brehm...* Jena, F. Mauke's verlag (A. Schenkk), 1885.

Weber cites a biographical sketch of Oviedo on pp. XXIII ff.

125. Caddeo, Rinaldo. [Review of Rómulo D. Carbia's; *Superchería en la historia del descubrimiento de América*] *Le opere e i giorni,* Milan, March 1, 1930. Pp. 47-56.

Caddeo edited what has come to be regarded as the standard modern edition of Ferdinand Columbus' *Life of the Admiral* (q. v.). This review triggered a heated polemic in the pages of *Nosotros.*

126. Caddeo, Rinaldo. «Sobre Fernando Colón y el Padre las Casas. El señor Carbia en favor de Oviedo. Oviedo contra el señor Carbia.» *Nosotros* (Buenos Aires) *LXIX.* Pp. 105-111.

Carbia considered *The Life of the Admiral...* attributed to Ferdinand Columbus a forgery, suggested, on strength of passages which are highly uncomplimentary to Oviedo, that the author might have been either Bartolomé de las Casas or Hernán Pérez de Oliva. Caddeo defends the authenticity of Ferdinand's authorship.

127. Carbia, Rómulo D. *La Crónica oficial de las Indias Occidentales.* Buenos Aires, Ediciones Buenos Aires, 1940. («Edición definitiva», the first edition appeared at La Plata in 1934.)

Points out that Oviedo was not first official «Cronista Mayor» of the Indies, but one of a number of official chroniclers.

128. Carbia, Rómulo D. «Fernández de Oviedo, Las Casas y el señor Caddeo.» *Nosotros* (Buenos Aires) LXX. 1930. Pp. 90-95.

An ill-tempered reply to Caddeo's article cited above.

129. Carbia, Rómulo D. «Fernando Colón, el P. Las Casas, un señor Caddeo y yo.» *Nosotros* (Buenos Aires) *LXVIII.* Pp. 59-73.

Reaction to Caddeo's review of the *Superchería.*

130. Carbia, Rómulo D. *La superchería en la historia del descubrimiento de América.* Buenos Aires, V. de la Plata, 1929.

The theory of the authorship of *Le Historie delle vita di Cristoforo Colombo...* advanced in this book touched off the debate with Caddeo reflected in preceding entries.

131. Cardenal Iracheta, Manuel. *Vida de Gonzalo Pizarro,* Madrid, Ediciones Cultura Hispánica, 1953.

«Esfuerzo de reivindicar la figura de Gonzalo Pizarro». Oviedo is among authorities cited.

132. C[ardenal], V. M. [Review of Alvarez López edition of *Sumario*] *Revista de Filología Española,* XXVI, (1942), pp. 118-119.

133. Carles, Rubén Darío. *220 Años del período colonial en Panamá.* 2.da ed. Panamá, Imprenta Nacional, 1959.

134. Carriazo, Juan de Mata. «Amor y moralidad bajo los Reyes Católicos.» *Revista de Archivos, Bibliotecas y Museos. LX.* Madrid, 1954.

Based on an unpublished xvii century manuscript in the Biblioteca Colombina, «*Algunos elogios y relaciones de personas y linajes* sacados de los *Diálogos* que escribió Gonzalo Fernández de Oviedo y Valdés, cronista del emperador Carlos V y criado de los Reyes Católicos.»

«Como narrador y como autor de retratos y biografías, Oviedo está en la línea y casi a la altura de nuestros grandes cronistas: Ayala, Guzmán y Pulgar. Pero así como no siempre mantiene la misma calidad literaria de sus antecesores y modelos, aunque a veces no les va en zaga, en algo les aventaja, y es en curiosidad nunca satisfecha, y en prodigiosa facundia. Curioso hasta la indiscreción y parlero hasta la prolijidad, todo quiere saberlo y todo quiere decirlo, sin miedo a las repeticiones y sin detenerse ni ante los secretos de la alcoba. Además el campo de sus experiencias personales fue dilatadísimo, como el de pocos hombres en toda la historia de la Humanidad.» (p. 54).

135. Carriazo, Juan de Mata. «Retratos literarios de la Corte de los Reyes Católicos.» *Archivo Hispalense.* 2da época. 77. Seville, 1956. Pp. 1-22.

136. Carriazo, Juan de Mata. «Tres cortesanos de los Reyes Católicos: Gonzalo Chacón, Gutierre de Cárdenas y don Diego Hurtado de Mendoza, semblanzas ejemplares de Gonzalo Fernández de Oviedo.» *Clavileño. II.* Madrid, 1951. Pp. 9-18.

Based on Colombina manuscript cited above.

137. Las Casas, Fr. Bartolomé de. «ESTAS SON LAS REPLICAS QUE EL OBISPO DE CHIAPA HACE CONTRA las soluciones de las doce objeciones que el doctor Sepúlveda hizo contra el *Sumario* de la su dicha *Apología.*» [in Vol. V. *Obras...*, Madrid, Real Academia Española, 1958. Pp. 329 ff. (*Biblioteca de Autores Españoles* CX)].

«Y lo que más perjudica la persona del reverendo doctor entre personas prudentes y temerosas de Dios, y que tienen noticia ocular de las Indias, es allegar y traer por autor irrefragable a Oviedo en falsísima *Historia* que llamó *general,* como haya sido uno de los tiranos robadores y destruidores de los indios, según él mismo confiesa en el prólogo de su primera parte, columna 6, y en el libro 6, cap. 8, y por ende, de los indios capital enemigo. Júzguese por los prudentes si para contra los indios es idóneo testigo. A éste, empero, llama el doctor grave y diligente cronista, porque lo halló a favor de paladar para socorro de la necesidad de verdades en que se ponía, estando aquella *Historia* poco más llena de hojas que de mentiras.»

138. Las Casas, Fr. Bartolomé de. *Historia de las Indias.* Ed. Agustín Millares Carlo y estudio preliminar de Lewis Hanke. Mexico-Buenos Aires. Fondo de Cultura Económica, 1951. 3 vols. (first published Madrid, 1875-76, reprinted in Mexico two years later.)

According to Las Casas' will this was not to be published for at least forty years after his death. Oviedo on several occasions twits the Bishop of Chiapa for his failure to issue the history on which he was reported to be working while there were still alive eye-witnesses to the events described. And some bibliographers credit the delay in the printing of the second and third part of the *Historia general...* to Las Casas' malice.

The *Indice analítico* to the present edition of Las Casas *Historia* de Indias, which erroneously dates Oviedo's arrival in the Indies as 1614, lists over thirty references to Oviedo or his writings in the text. Most of these are uncomplimentary.

There is no evidence in the Alcaide's printed works that he ever saw the Lascasian tracts which were printed during his own lifetime notably the *Brevissima relacion de la destruycion de las Indias...* Seville, Sebastián Trugillo, 1552.

139. Castañeda, Vicente. «Don Fernando de Aragón, duque de Calabria. Apuntes biográficos.» *Revista de Archivos, Bibliotecas y Museos.* XXV. Madrid, 1911. Pp. 268-286.

Notes on the patronto whom Oviedo dedicated his *Claribalte*.

140. Castellanos, Juan. ...*Elegías de varones ilustres de Indias.* Madrid, M. Rivadeneyra, 1857. (*Biblioteca de Autores Españoles, IV.*) The first complete edition. The *Primera parte de las Elegías de Varones ilustres...* was printed at Madrid by Vda. de Alonso Gómez in 1589.

Muna Lee has pointed Castellanos' indebtedness to Oviedo for much of the factual material used in his verses.

141. Castillero R., Ernesto J. «Gonzalo Fernández de Oviedo, veedor en Tierra-Firme.» *Revista de Indias.* XVII. (Jul-Dec. 1957). Pp. 521-540.

Adds little to knowledge gleaned from other sources concerning this period in our historian's life.

142. Castro, Américo. *The Structure of Spanish History.* Princeton, Princeton University Press, 1954. (Revision, in English, of the same author's *España en su historia* published in 1948).

Cites Oviedo as to the number and diversity of peoples subject to the Spanish crown.

143. *Catálogo de la Colección de Don Juan Bautista Muñoz. Prólogo de A. Ballesteros Beretta. Advertencia de M. G. del* C[ampillo]. Madrid, Real Academia de la Historia, 1954. 3 vols.

Detailed descriptions of manuscripts in the Muñoz Collection of the Library of the Royal Academy of History in Madrid. In addition to mss. of the *Historia general...* listed above this Catalog mentions some thirty other documents dealing with Oviedo.

144. Cejador y Frauca, Julio. *Historia de la lengua y literatura castellana. II.* 2da ed. Madrid, Librería y Casa Editorial Hernando, S. A., 1928. Pp. 52-55.

«[Oviedo] Es el Plinio americano y el más transparente historiador de aquella época... mayormente en lo tocante a las primeras conquistas del Nuevo Mundo. No abarca como filósofo en conjunto los grandes acontecimientos; pero en cambio se detiene en pormenores, que otros menospreciarían, pintándonos con mayor viveza los hechos, los hombres y los objetos, sin faltarle de vez en cuando el calor que le comunica la visión de cosas tan maravillosas, de tan grandes acaecimientos y de tan pasmosas empresas.» (p. 53).

145. Cerwin, Herbert. *Bernal Díaz. Historian of the Conquest.* Norman, University of Oklahoma Press, 1963.

Especially interesting for picture of life in the Spanish colonies in years following the conquest of Mexico.

146. Céspedes del Castillo, Guillermo. «La defensa militar del istmo de Panamá a fines del siglo xvii y comienzos del xviii.» *Anuario de Estudios Americanos, IX.*

Strategic importance of Santa María del Antigua.

147. Chamberlain, Robert S. *The Conquest of Honduras 1502-1550.* Washington, D. C. Carnegie Institution of Washington, 1953.

148. Chandler, Richard E. and Kessel Schwartz. *A New History of Spanish Literature.* Baton Rouge, La., Louisiana State University Press, c. 1961.

Cf. p. 461: «Oviedo has been criticized for lack of style and carlessness, verbosity and faulty organization, but no one could disagree that his account is a prodigious repository of factual information. Writing in the old, rambling, chronicling style, he extensively went into a description of the land, the Indians, their life, dress, and customs, the animals, the trees and plants, and many other aspects of the American scene. His books are not prized as literature, but as accurate firsthand documentation on the conquest and the subjugated peoples, which has been useful to later generations.

149. Chardon, Carlos E. *Los naturalistas en la América Latina.* Ciudad Trujillo, R. D., Editora del Caribe, 1949.

Chauveton, Urbano V. Benzoni, Girolamo.

150. Chinchilla Aguilar, Ernesto. «Algunos aspectos de la obra de Oviedo.» *Revista de Historia de América. XXVIII.* (Mexico, 1949).

An interesting and generally valid appraisal of Oviedo's concept of history supported by quotations from Ríos edition of the *Historia general*... Chinchilla has a higher opinion of the Chronicler's style than many critics, for he calls him «uno de los grandes prosistas españoles del siglo xvi» (p. 321). The biographical sketch wich concludes the article is dated and erroneously give the date of death as 1579.

151. Clemencín, Diego. «Noticia y descripción de las Quincuagenas compuestas por Gonzalo Fernández de Oviedo». *Memorias de la Real Academia de la Historia.* VI. 1821. Pp. 221-36.

The reference is here as given by Simón Díaz. I have been unable to consult the text. But a number of other authorities refer to Clemencín's *Elogios de Isabel la Católica*, a speech read before the Academy on July 31, 1807, and reprinted in this same volume (there had been a first edition in the previous year). The *Elogio*... is reputed to draw heavily on the *Batallas y quincuagenas*... hence the title above may be in error, or Don Diego may have been one of a number of distinguished historians, including Ticknor and Prescott, to confuse the similar titles of *La Quincuagenas* and *Las Batallas y quincuagenas*...

152. *Colección de documentos inéditos para la historia de Ibero-America.* Madrid-Barcelona-Buenos Aires, Compañía Ibero-Americana de Publicaciones (S. A.), n. d., 14 vols.

Vol. XIV (*T. III Catálogo de los Fondos Americanos del Archivo de Protocolos de Sevilla*) describes three documents relating to Oviedo (171, 613, 639).

153. *Colección de libros y documentos referentes a la historia de América.* Madrid, Victoriano Suárez, 1904-1929. 21 vols.

General background only.

154. *Colección de Documentos inéditos relativos al descubrimiento, conquista y colonización de las posesiones españolas en América y Oceania, sacados en su mayor parte del Real Archivo de Indias.* Madrid, [imprint varies], 1864-84. 1st series. 42 vols.

154a. *Colección de Documentos inéditos relativos al descubrimiento, conquista y organización de las antiguas posesiones españolas de Ultramar.* Madrid, Real Academia de la Historia, 1884-1932. 2nd series. 25 vols.

According to Schaeffer's *Indice...* ten volumes of the first series and six of the second reproduce documents relating to Oviedo.

155. Collel, Jaime. *Fray Bernardo Boyl Primer Apóstol de América.* Vich, Imp. de L. Anglada, 1929.

Oviedo gives an entertaining account of Fr. Bernardo's differences with the First Admiral in chapter 13 of the Second Book of the *Historia general...*

156. Colón, Fernando. *Historie della Vite dell' Ammiraglio D. Christoforo Colombo suo padre...* Venice, Francesco de Franceschi Sanese, 1571.

An Italian translation by Alonso Ulloa of a lost Spanish original. There have been numerous editions and translations since, the best modern one being considered that of Rinaldo Caddeo, Milan, 1930. The authenticity of authorship is no longer questioned. Chapter 10 contains a sharp refutation of Oviedo's theory that the Indies had formerly belonged to the Spanish crown. The animosity displayed towards our Alcaide having led some authorities in the past to consider the *Vite...* a forgery by Las Casas or some other enemy of the historian. Consulted in the English translation by Benjamin Keen: *The Life of the Admiral Christopher Columbus by his son Ferdinand.* (New Brunswick, N. J., Rutgers University Press, 1959). This edition reproduces several of the woodcuts from the 1547 edition of the *Historia general...*

157. Cortés, Hernando. *Ferdinandi Cortesii von dem Newen Hispanica... zwo... Historien... Darzu auch von vilen andern Landtschafften Indiae, so erfunden von dem 1536 bis auf das 42 Jar...* Augsburg, Philipp Vlhart, 1550.

As we have pointed out elsewere Oviedo somewhat grudgingly used Cortés *Cartas de relación* as a source for his Historia general... This present edition of a German translation of two of the letters and other histories also contains a letter from the Alcaide dated Santo Domingo, Jaunary 20, 1543.

158. Cortés, Vicente. «Los indios caribes en el siglo xvi.» [in *Procedings of the Thirty-second International Conference of Americanists*. Copenhagen, Munkgaard, 1958. Pp. 726-731].

159. Dahlgren, Erik Wilhelm. *Map of the World by Alonso de Santa Cruz*. Stockholm, 1892.

Cited by Harrisse on the importance of Oviedo in reconstructing Cabot's route to La Plata.

160. Dantín Cereceda, Juan, ed. *Exploradores y conquistadores de Indias*, Madrid, Tip. de Archivos, 1934.

According to Olivera contains selections from Oviedo not further specified (pp. 48-53).

161. Dantín Cereceda, Juan, ed. *Historiadores de los siglos xvi y xvii*, Madrid, Biblioteca literaria del estudiante, 1922.

Reported to contain selections from Oviedo.

162. Davenport, Herbert. «The Expedition of Pánfilo de Narvaez by Gonzalo Fernández de Oviedo y Valdez». *Southwestern Historical Quarterly*. October 1923, January, April, July, October 1924. XXVII & XXVIII.

A translation of Oviedo's version of the Alvar Nuñez Cabeza de Vaca report sent to our chronicler from La Habana. In the *Historia general...* he refers to discrepancies between this account and that published at Zaragoza by Nuñez in 1542.

163. Delgado, Jaime, ed. *Los viajes de Colón*. [selections from the *Historia general...*] Madrid, Editorial Atlas, n. d. [*Colección Cisneros*, LXXV].

164. Díaz del Castillo, Bernal. *Historia Verdadera de la Conquista de la Nueva España*. Mexico, Porrúa, n. d. 2 vols. (First edition Madrid, 1605).

Díaz says he came to the New World with Pedrarias Dávila in 1514. This would have made him a passenger in the same fleet which brought Oviedo, but there is no evidence in the work of either that the two historians, at that time a young fortune hunter and a mature royal official, were ever personally acquainted, nor do they mention one another in their respective writings. However Henry Raup Wagner has suggested that Díaz's account of the Grijalva expedition may be based on the *Historia general...*

165. Diffie, Baily W. *Latin American Civilization: Colonial Period.* Harrisburg, Pa., Stackpole Sons, c. 1945.

Oviedo cited on pp. 39, 40, 94, 101, 147-148, 267, 401 & 517.

166. D'Olwer, Luis Nicolau. *Cronistas de las culturas precolombinas.* Mexico, Fondo de Cultura Económica, 1963.

Biographical sketch on. pp. 68-72 follows data given by Ríos, lists dat of printing of Book XX of *Historia general...* as 1552 on authority of Pinelo. There follow extracts from the *Historia general...*: «De las costumbres de Haiti», pp. 73-80; «De la isla de Jamaica», pp. 81-82; «La gente del golfo de Nicaragua», pp. 355-356; «Diversas maneras de areytos», pp. 357-364; «Otras costumbres», pp. 365-367; «De los cunacueva del Istmo y otras gentes vecinas», pp. 371-397. D'Olwer also includes selections from Alvar Nuñez Cabeza de Vaca, Rodrigo Rangel, Hernán Cortés, Francisco de Xerez, Gaspar de Carvajar and other writers whose works were used by Oviedo, but he admits that the latter is «quien da el mayor acopio de... noticias [de aquellos pueblos].» (p. 7).

167. Elliot, L. E. *Central America.* London, Methuen & Co., Ltd., c. 1924.

See pp. 153-154 for citation of Oviedo in reference to Nicaragua.

168. Ellis, George Edward. «Las Casas and the relations of the Spaniards to the Indians... [with a critical essay on sources of information and editorial note].» (Chapter 5, Vol. II, Justin Winsor's *Narative and critical history of America,* Boston and New York, Houghton, Mifflin & Co., 1886. Pp. 299-348).

Illustrations include a reproduction of the frontispiece of the *Sumario...* and Oviedo's coat of arms from the 1535 edition of the *Historia general...* The critical note cites Ticknor and Harrisse, goes on to add: «In the estimate commonly made of Oviedo there is allowed him but scant scholarship, little power of discrimination, —as shown in his giving at times as much weight to hearsay evidence as to established testimony—, a curious and shrewd insight which sometimes, with his industry, leads him to a better balance of authorities than might be expected from his deficient judgement. He resources of material were uncommon, his use of them is generally tedious...»

169. Esteve Barba, Francisco. *Historiografía indiana.* Madrid, Editorial Gredos (1964).

Excellent sketch and appraisal which summarize most recent investigations, pp. 59-75. Oviedo is considered in light of his personality, his biography, as an historian, as a naturalist and as an ethnographer. The opening pages of Esteve Barba's sketch of Las Casas (i. e. pp. 75-77) also compare and contrast the Chronicler with his arch-rival the Bishop of Chiapa.

170. Endress Hepp, Alfredo. «Dos cronistas del descubrimiento de Chile: Christobal de Molina y Gonzalo Fernández de Oviedo.» *Boletín de la Academia Chilena de Historia XI*. Santiago de Chile. Pp. 49-70.

171. Ezguerra, R. [Review of Enrique Alvarez López's edition of the *Sumario*] *Revista de Indias*, III. Pp. 383-384.

172. Fernández Alvarez, Manuel. *Carlos V Memorias*. Madrid, Ediciones Cultura Hispánica, 1960.

Of interest because of the Emperor's itinerary (p. 48 ff), as Oviedo usually attempted to follow the Court on his visits to Spain.

173. Fernández de Navarrete, Eustaquio. *Historia de Juan Sebastián Elcano*, Victoria, Imprenta de los Hijos de Mantili, 1872.

Appendix xvii cites Oviedo as to final resting place of the «famous ship *Victoria*».

174. Fernández de Enciso, Martín, *el bachiller*. *Summa de geografía*, Seville, Jacobo Cromberger, 1519.

A book which our chronicler must have owned and cherished. He tells us «El bachiller Enciso... era mi amigo.»

175. Ferrando Pérez, Roberto. *Descubrimientos españoles en el Pacífico. Virreinato del Perú. Siglos XVI-XVII*.

Unpublished doctoral dissertation mentioned by its author in the article listed below.

176. Ferrando Pérez, Roberto. «Fernández de Oviedo y el conocimiento del Mar del Sur». *Revista de Indias*, XVII (Jul-Dec. 1957), pp. 469-482.

Oviedo's concept of probable coastline north of New Spain was more accurate than that of many of his contemporaries.

177. Fiske, John. *The Discovery of America*. New York, Houghton, Mifflin and Co., 1898. 2 vols.

Vol. II mentions Oviedo anent the discovery of Honduras (p. 70) and his relations with Pedrarias in Darien (pp. 377-8).

178. Fitzmaurice-Kelly, James. *A New History of Spanish Literature...* New York, Oxford University Press, 1926.

Judgement of Oviedos, based largely on Menéndez Pelayo, concludes: «These [works] have no literary quality, but they contain observations of some scientific value» (pp. 204-205).

179. Fracastoro, Girolamo. *Syphilis sive de Morbo Gallico*, Verona, 1530.

A long Latin poem in three parts on origin and treatment of syphilis. It has been alleged that the author's statement on the American origin of syphilis and the use of guaiacum as a specific for treatment may derive from Oviedo. The chronicler apparently at least knew of Fracastoro (or Fracastor) and refers to him in the *Historia general...* as an astronomer.

180. Friede, Juan, ed. *Documentos inéditos para la historia de Colombia*. Bogotá, Academia de Historia, 1955-56. 4 vols.

Cf. p. 73, Vol. I, for capitulation granting Oviedo right to trade along coast of Cartagena.

181. Friede, Juan. *Los Welser en la conquista de Venezuela*. Caracas-Madrid, Edime, 1961.

Oviedo cited on pp. 14, 16, 48, 98, 104, 107-109, 147, 150, 176, 196, 233, 266, 279, 283, 289, 300, 332, 333, 358, 372, 384, 497 and 511.

182. Fueter, Eduard. *Histoire de l'Historiographie Moderne*. Paris, Felix Alcan, 1914. (First published in German in 1911).

See p. 369 for citicism of Oviedo's method of reporting conflicting accounts of the same event.

183. Fullana, Fr. Luis. «Historia de San Miguel de los Reyes.» *Boletín de la Academia de la Historia, CVI* (1). Pp. 151-196 and *CVII* (2). Pp. 693-740. Madrid, 1935.

In his second installment Fr. Luis cites biographical data concerning Fernando de Aragón, Duke of Calabria, taken from a mss. of Oviedo's *Batallas y Quincuagenas* in the Biblioteca de Salamanca.

184. Gallo, Ugo and Giuseppe Bellini. *Storia della letteratura ispanoamericana. Seconda edizione.* Milan, Nuova Accademia Editrice, col. 1958.

Sketch on p. 16 based largely on Menéndez Pelayo. «Quest' opera ha i meriti della testimonianza; tratta dalle prime grandi conquiste spagnole: Antille, Messico e Perú. I pregi letterari che mancano ad essa sono, invece, riscontrabili nell'altra *Historia general de las Indias* dovuta alla penna di Antonio De Herrera y Tordesillas.»

185. García, José Gabriel. *Compendio de la Historia de Santo Domingo.* 3ra ed., Santo Domingo, Imp. de García Hmnos, 193.

Oviedo one of sources for Vol. I.

186. García, Julio César. «Gonzalo Fernández de Oviedo y Valdés.» *Boletín de Historia y antigüedades* (Bogotá), *XLIV*, (516/18), oct.-dic., 1957. Pp. 511-538.

187. García, Julio César. «El primer cronista y el primer historiador: Gonzalo Fernández de Oviedo y Valdés.» *Universidad de Antioquia.* (Medellín), XXXIV (134), jul-sept. 1958. Pp. 471-496.

188. Garibay y Zamalloa, Estevan de. *Los XL libros d'el compendio de las Chronicas...* Antwerp, Christophoro Plantino, 1571.

Work highly esteemed by Harrisse, Washington Irving and Southey.

189. Gasteazoro, Carlos Manuel. *Introducción al estudio de la historia de Panamá... Tomo I.* Mexico, Azteca, S. A., 1956.

190. Gerbi, Antonello. «El *Claribalte* de Oviedo.» *Fénix, Revista de la Biblioteca Nacional.* VI. Lima, 1949. Pp. 378-390.

191. Giménez Fernández, Manuel. *Bartolomé de las Casas...*, Seville, Escuela de Estudios Hispano-americanos, 1953-1960. 2 vols. [to date].

Invaluable for an understanding of the time. But like most partisans of Las Casas, Giménez is hostile to Oviedo whom he terms a «pseudo-capitán».

192. Giménez Fernández, Manuel. «El Estatuto de la tierra de Casas.» *Anales de la Universidad Hispalense. Año X.* 1949. Pp. 27-101.

193. G. O. M. «Galería de historiadores neogranadinos: Gonzalo Hernández de Oviedo y Valdés.» *Boletin de historia y antigüedades de Bogotá.* XXI. 1934. Pp. 3-5.

194. Gómara, Francisco López de. *The Annals of the Emperor Charles V... Spanish Text and English Translation...* by Roger Bigelow Merriman... Oxford, Clarendon Press, 1912.

Apparently first publication of a mss. which Gallardo in 1888 mentioned as being in the Biblioteca Cardrera.

195. Gómara, Francisco López de. *Primera y segunda parte de la Historia general de las Indias... ata el año de 1551. Con la conquista de México y de la nueua España...* Zaragoza, Agustín Millán, 1552.

Washington Irving believed that Gómara drew much of his information about the discovery from Oviedo.

196. Haebler, Konrad. *Prosperidad y decadencia económica de España durante el siglo xvi.* Madrid, Vda. e Hijos de Tello, 1899.

197. Hallenack, Cleve. *Alvar Nuñez Cabeza de Vaca. The Journey and Route.* Glendale, Cal., Arthur H. Clark, 1940.

Cf. p. 23 regarding the difference between Oviedo's account and that published by Alvar Núñez at Zamora in 1542. Vallodolid, 1555, a difference on which Oviedo himself remarked.

198. Haring, Clarence H. *The Spanish Empire in America.* New York, Oxford University Press, 1947.

Lists Oviedo among sources consulted.

199. Harrington, N. R. *Cuba before Columbus.* New York, Heye Foundation, 1921. [Indian Notes and Monographs, Museum of the American Indian].

Oviedo cited on pp. 62, 129, 138, 142, 416.

200. Harrisse, Henry. *Biblioteca americana vetustissima.* New York, G. P. Philes, 1866. (Reprinted at Paris by Maisonneuve, 1922).

A standard reference work, listing 304 titles relating to the New World printed between 1492 and 1551. Sketch of Oviedo on p. 340.

201. Harrisse, Henry. *D. Fernando Colón Historiador de su padre...* Seville, Imprenta de D. R. Tarasco, 1871. [*Sociedad de Bibliófilos Andaluces*, 1ra ser., III].

Maintains that Ferdinand Columbus did *not* write the life of his father, largely on the strength of lack of reference to it in records of the Biblioteca Colombina and the impossibility of Don Luis' personal delivery of the mss. to Italy. Harrisse subsequently modified his position in the controversy after publication of Las Casas *Historia de Indias*. There are references to Oviedo on pp. 13, 43, 45 and 86.

202. Harrisse, Henry. *John Cabot the Discoverer of North America.* London, Benjamin Franklin Stevens, 1896.

Numerous citations from Oviedo who was personally acquainted with Cabot and familiar with the work of contemporary chart makers. There is a discussion of his role as «Historiographer Royal for the Indies» on pp. 201-205.

203. Helps, Arthur. *The Spanish Conquest of America...*, London-New York, John Lane, 1900-04. (First edition, 1855), 4 vols.

References to Oviedo in all four volumes, chiefly in volume I.

204. Herrera, Antonio de. *Historia general de los hechos de los castellanos en las islas y Tierra-Firme del Mar Océano.* Asunción del Paraguay, Editorial Guarnanía, 1944-47. 10 vols. (First edition, Madrid, 1601).

The editor, J. Natalicio González has also edited the only American edition of Oviedo's *Historia general...* and in his prolog to present work points out that only a little patience is needed to discover Herrera's debt to Oviedo. Nevertheless, Herrera knew only the first part of Oviedo's work, in a famous polemic with Pedrarias' grandson affirmed that Oviedo had not composed a second or third part of his *General History...*

205. Hilton, Ronald. *Handbook of Hispanic Source Materials...* 2nd Ed. Stanford, Cal., Stanford University Press, 1956.

Mentions Oviedo mss. in the Huntington Library, including autograph mss. of certain books of the *Historia general...* described above, first edition in the Library of Congress and an early French translation in the library of Florida State University.

206. Humboldt, Alexander von. *Cosmos, o ensayo de una descripción física del mundo...* Madrid, Est. tip. de D. Ramón Rodríguez de Rivera, Editor, 1851-52. 2 vols.

See Chapter 6, Volume II: «Desarrollo de la idea del cosmos en los siglos XV y XVI» p. 356 ff.

207. Humboldt, Alexander von. *Histoire de la Géographie du Nouveau Continent...* Paris, Théodore Morgand, n. d. 5 vols. (First edition: Paris 1836-39.)

Humboldt apparently knew Oviedo only through such secondary sources as Ramusio, Muñoz and Herrera.

208. Hurtado, Juan and J. de la Serna and Angel González-Palencia. *Historia de la literatura española. Sexta edición...* Madrid, Saeta, 1949.

The sketch of Oviedo (p. 380) is distinguished by egregious errors of fact and judgement, e. g., Oviedo is termed a *page* of Prince John; the *Sumario...* is confused with the First Part of the *Historia general...* the 1535, 1547, and 1557 editions of which are ignored. *Claribalte* is mistakenly dated 1510 and attributed to «su homónimo, alias de Sobrepeña, vecino de Madrid.»

209. Iglesia, Ramón. «Bernal Díaz del Castillo y el popularismo en la historiografía española». *Tierra Firme,* 1935 (4). Pp. 5-18.

Bernal Díaz' attitude towards Gómara is compared with that of Oviedo towards Peter Martyr.

210. *Indice de la colección de don Luis de Salazar y Castro.* Madrid, Real Academia de la Historia, 1949-63. XXXII vols.

Among Oviedo mss. described are a copy of his *Libro de linajes y armas...* (v. XI, pp. 287-299); of the ubiquitous *Libro de la cámara* (XXVII, p. 361); and the remains of an autograph ms. of parts of the *Historia general...* found in an inventory of 1928 to be badly mutilated (XXI, pp. 309-312).

211. Irving, Washington. *The Life and Voyages of Christopher Columbus. ...Author's Revised Edition.* G. P. Putnam's Sons, 1868. 3 vols.

States that Gómara's story of Columbus and the unknown pilot is «manifestly from Oviedo» (III, p. 416).

212. Ispizúa, Segundo de. *Los Vascos en América, III... Panamá, ...IV Perú...* Madrid, Tip. «La Itálica», 1917.

Various references to *Historia general...* and the first edition of the *Sumario*.

213. Jane, Cecil (trans. & ed.). *The Voyages of Christopher Columbus...* London, Argonaut Press, 1930.

Oviedo cited on pp. 10, 11, 12, 56, 58, 65, 80, 102, 329, 330, 331 and 333.

214. Jos, Emiliano. «Fernando Colón y su historia del almirante». *Revista de Historia de América,* IX Aug. 1940. Pp. 5-29.

Mentions Fernando's personal friendship with Oviedo and his appreciation of the *Sumario* as well as the probable role of certain assertions in the *Primera Parte* of the *Historia general...* in influencing him to undertake a biography of his father.

215. Keniston, Hayward. *Francisco de los Cobos, Secretary of the Emperor Charles V.* Pittsburgh, Pa., University of Pittsburgh Press, n. d.

Draws heavily on Oviedo as the one contemporary historian who knew Cobos as a boy, cites not only *Historia general...* but *Quincuagenas* (published and unpublished portions), the *Libro de linajes...* and the *Relación de lo sucedido en la prisión del rey de Francia...*

216. Kirkpatrick, F. A. *The Spanish Conquistadors.* London, A. & C. Black, 1934.

Numerous citations of Oviedo concerning Columbus, Balboa, the Darien, De Soto, Peru, Almagro's expedition to Chile, Pizarro, Orellana, etc.

217. Krushinsky, Martin. «Oviedo on the conquest of New Spain.» *Records American Catholic Historical Society,* XXIV (3), Sept. 1953. Pp. 155-65.

Concludes that Oviedo adds little to the *Cartas* of Cortés and other well-known accounts. It will be recalled that in his *Historia general...* (p. 8, Vol. IV, Madrid, 1959 ed.) the chronicler complains of the Marquis del Valle's failure to cooperate «Y escribí y avisé al Marqués del Valle, don Hernando Cortés, que me enviase la [relación] suya, conforme con lo que subcesivamente mandaba [el Emperador], y remitióme a unas cartas misivas que le escribió a Su Majestad, de lo sucedido en aquella conquista, e no curó de más...».

218. Lafuente, Modesto. *Historia general de España... continuada... por don Juan Valera.* Barcelona, Montaner y Simón, 1887-90. 25 vols.

A standard work on Spanish history. Extensive use of the Ríos' edition *Historia general...* in volumes 7, 8 and 9.

219. Lamb, Ursula S. «Una biografía contemporánea y una carta de fray Nicolás de Ovando, Gobernador de las Indias.» *Revista de Estudios Extremeños* VII (3 & 4) 1951. Pp. 693-707.

Sketch of Oviedo from *Las Quincuagenas...* and letter from New York Public Library.

220. Lamb, Ursula, S. *Fray Nicolás de Ovando, gobernador de Indias* (1501-1509), Madrid, Consejo Superior de Investigaciones Científicas, 1956.

At least two dozen references to or citations of Oviedo.

221. Leguizamón, Julio A. *Historia de la literatura hispanoamericana. Tomo I.* Buenos Aires, Editoriales reunidas, S. A., 1945.

Mentions only the *Historia general...* (pp. 123-124). Says that the author «... no se acredita como un hombre de letras, a pesar de intentarlo. Su mérito radica en la pertinaz memoria que mantiene vivo el recuerdo de cuando vivió o conoció, y que prolijamente traslada a sus escritos.» ... «Hombre de acción, escribió historia vivida, veta riquísima de noticias útiles, imprescindible necesidad para el conocimiento de la conquista.»

222. Lee, Muna. «Juan de Castellanos in the Perspective of 350 Years.» *Actas del XXXIII Congreso Internacional de Americanistas.* San José de Costa Rica, 1959. II, pp. 859-872.

«It is interesting to observe in how many instances Castellanos takes a basic account from Oviedo but adds details as he is able to pick them up to fill in the gaps or otherwise interpret of vivfy the narrative.»

223. López de Meneses, Amada. «Andrea Navagero, traductor de Gonzalo Fernández de Oviedo.» *Revista de Indias* XV (71). Pp. 63-72.

Suggests Navagero, who was Venetian Ambassador to the Spanish court at the time it appeared, as translator of Oviedo's *Sumario...*

224. López de Meneses, Amada. «Gonzalo Fernández de Oviedo, traductor del *Corbaccio*. «*Revista de la Biblioteca, Archivo y Museo del Ayuntamiento de Madrid*. Madrid, 1935. pp. 111-112.

Cites one of two or three extant documents which seem to indicate that the chronicler had prepared a translation of Boccacio's *Il corbaccio* for publication ca. 1526.

225. Lowery, Woodbury. *The Spanish Settlements within the present limits of the United States 1513-1561*. New York - London, G. P. Putnam's Sons, 1901.

A standard work which draws on Oviedo for account of the Ayllon expedition (pp. 154-161).

226. Lozoya, Marqués de. *Vida del Segoviano Rodrigo de Contreras Gobernador de Nicaragua* (1534-1544). Toledo, Imp. Ed. Católica Toledana, 1920.

Mentions Oviedo as a personal acquaintance of Contreras and an impartial witness.

227. Madariaga, Salvador de. *Christopher Columbus*. New York, Macmillan, 1940.

Cites Oviedo as «one of the earliest historian of the Indies» (p. 34), «a well-informed and detached historian» (p. 344). Also see pp. 56, 60, 112, 162, 200, 263, 278, 344.

228. Manzano Manzano, Juan. *La incorporación de las Indias a la corona de Castilla*. Madrid, Ediciones Cultura Hispánica, 1948.

229. March, José Miguel. ed. *Niñez y juventud de Felipe II. Documentos inéditos...* (*1527-1547*). Madrid, Ministerio de Asuntos Exteriores, 1941-42, 2 vols.

No reference to Oviedo, but interesting for portrait of the prince to whom he dedicated his *Libro de la cámara* and to whom he addressed many of his letters.

230. Mariana, P. Juan de. *Historia general de España... y la continuación de Miñano, traducida... y adicionada... una narración de sucesos hasta 1833*. Barcelona, Francisco Oliva, 1839, 10 vols.

One of the classics of Spanish historiography, first published in Latin at Toledo by Pedro Rodríguez in 1601.
Consult volumes V & VI of the present edition.

231. Markham, Sir Clements R. *The Conquest of New Granada.* New York, E. P. Dutton and Company, 1912.

232. Marrero Aristy, Ramón. *La República Dominicana. Origen y destino del pueblo cristiano más antiguo de América.* Ciudad Trujillo, Editora del Caribe, 1958. 2 vols.

Extensive citation of Oviedo in earlier chapters of Volume I.

233. Maticorena Estrada, Miguel. «Una traducción desconcida de Oviedo.» *Estudios americanos. LXVII.* April 1957.

Concerning the putative translation of *Il corbaccio* under the title of *Laberinto de amor.* This had been reported by Amada López de Meneses more than twenty years earlier.

234. Matilla Tascón, Antonio. *Los viajes de Julián Gutiérrez al Golfo de Urubá.* Seville, Escuela de Estudios Hispano-Americanos, 1945.

Off-print on an article appearing on pp. 181-263, Vol. II, *Anuario de estudios americanos.*

235. Means, Philip Ainsworth. *The Spanish Main: Focus of Envy 1492-1700.* New York, Charles Scribner's Sons, 1935.

Oviedo is listed as one of sources.

236. Medina, José Toribio. *Vasco Núñez de Balboa.* Santiago de Chile, en casa del autor, 1913. 2 vols.

Volume II reproduces twelve documents dealing with Oviedo, three of them from his own pen.

237. Menéndez y Pelayo, Marcelino. *Antología de Poetas Líricos Castellanos.* Vol. III [*Obras completas...* XIX]. Santander, Aldus, 1944.

References to the household of Prince John as described in the *Libro de la cámara* on pp. 19 & 22.

238. Menéndez Pelayo, Marcelino. *Estudios Históricos* VII [*Obras completas...* XII]. Santander, Aldus, 1942.

On pp. 86-91 an inaccurate biographical sketch, based largely on Ríos. P. 106 cites Humboldt as to relative merit of Oviedo and Acosta as naturalists.

239. Menéndez Pelayo, Marcelino. *Estudios sobre el teatro de Lope de Vega. V.* [*Obras completas...* XXXIII]. Santander, Aldus, 1949.

Oviedo listed as one of two sources for Lope's *El nuevo mundo descubierto por Colón*. (The other is given as Gómara, who, according to Washington Irving «manifestly» based *his* account on Oviedo's.)

240. Menéndez Pelayo, Marcelino. *Historia de los Heterodoxos Españoles. VIII* [*Obras completas...* XLII], Santander, Aldus, 1948.

Cites Oviedo in Appendix II (p. 268) to effect that Indians on Hispaniola observed period of continence before mining gold and that Columbus ordered his men to confess and take communion in the same circumstances.

241. Menéndez Pelayo, Marcelino. *Historia de la Poesía Hispano-Americana I.* [*Obras completas...* XXVII], Santander, Aldus, 1948.

See pp. 287-290 for Oviedo's place in the colonial culture of Santo Domingo. Because of the «segunda rima» of the *Quincuagenas...* Menéndez considers him one of first Spanish-American poets, though an untalented one.

242. Menéndez Pelayo, Marcelino. *Orígenes de la novela. I. & III* [*Obras completas...* XIII & XV], Santander, Aldus, 1943.

I, p. 431 discussion of the *Claribalte*. III, p. 45. mentioned for his account of Becerril, the dog belonging to Juan Ponce de León.

243. Menéndez Pidal, Ramón. *Idea Imperial de Carlos V.* Buenos Aires, Espasa-Calpe, 1946 (First ed. 1941).

A lecture presented at the Institución Hispano-Cubana de Cultura and first published in the *Revista cubana* in 1937, subsequently issued independently by the Dirección de Cultura de la Secretaría de Educación, La Habana, 1938.

244. Merriman, Roger Bigelow. *The Rise of the Spanish Empire in the Old World and the New.* New York, Macmillan, 1918-1934. 4 vols.

Note volumes II and III.

245. Mexía, Pedro. *Historia del Emperador Carlos V.* Madrid, Espasa-Calpe, 1945. (The author died in 1551. First published by Deloffre in volume XLIV of the *Revue Hispanique*.)

Mexía was a fellow-chronicler and personal friend of Oviedo who speaks flatteringly of his *Silva de varia lección* (1540).

246. Milla, José (*alias* Salome Jil). *Historia de la América Central...* 2.da ed. Guatemala, C. A., Tip. Nacional, 1937. 2 vols. (First edition in 1879-97).

Uses Oviedo, particularly in volume I.

247. Miralles del Imperial y Gómez, Claudio. «Del linaje y armas del primer cronista de Indias.» *Revista de Indias XVI.* pp. 73-126.

Miralles adds little to our knowledge of the chronicler's antecedents, but gives an interesting discussion of his blazon, and a list of his blood descendants (through a daughter Juana, who married a nephew of Bishop Bastidas) down to the beginning of the present century. He also publishes a contemporary account of the circumstances of the Alcaide's death in the fortress of Santo Domingo, which should put to rest once and for all the frequently made assertion that he died in Valladolid. This latter document had been previously printed in a number of Cuban and Dominican journals.

248. Mirsky, Jeanette. *The Westward Crossings...* New York, Alfred A. Knopf, 1946.

Mentions Oviedo's accompaning Pedrarias (p. 73) and his report of oranges growing on Hispaniola (p. 106).

249. Monte y Tejada, Antonio del. *Historia del Santo Domingo.* 3.ra ed. Ciudad Trujillo, Impresora Dominicana, 1952-53. 3 vols. (First edition: Santo Domingo, 1891).

Includes report on Oviedo's death subsequently reproduced by Miralles and others.

Montoto, Santiago, ed. v. *Colección de Documentos inéditos para la historia de Ibero-América.*

250. Morales Padrón, Francisco. *Jamaica Española.* Sevilla, Consejo Superior de Investigaciones Científicas, 1952.

Cites Oviedo on pp. 26, 27, 41-43, 50 and 255-6.

251. Morales Padrón, Francisco. «Los grandes cronistas de Indias.» *Estudios americanos.* XIV (73-74). 1957. pp. 85-108.

Appraisal of Oviedo appears based on secondary sources: Chinchilla Aguilar, Amador de los Ríos, Peña y Cámara, and the editor of the Asunción edition of the *Historia general...* Natalicio González.

252. Morel-Fatio, A. «Sobre *Las Quinquagenas...*, ed. de don Vicente de la Fuente, t. 1.» *Revue Historique XXI.* pp. 179 ff.

Frequently mentioned review which is rather critical of La Fuente's editing.

253. Morison, Samuel Eliot. *Admiral of the Ocean Sea.* Boston, Little, Brown & Co., 1942.

Morison has a higher regard for Oviedo than that entertained by Prescott, praises his observations on flora and fauna and his chapters on navigation. However, he feels that Las Casas was a better narrative historian. (See sketch pp. 52-53). In the two volume edition of this work he draws on Oviedo for his discussion of the American origin of syphilis.

254. Morison, Samuel Eliot and Mauricio Obregon. *The Caribbean as Columbus Saw It.* Boston, Atlantic, Little, Brown, 1964.

In addition to fine aerial photos of the land which Oviedo, as well as Columbus, knew there are several reproductions of woodcuts from 1535 edition of the *Historia general...*

255. Morison, Samuel Eliot. *Christopher Columbus, Mariner.* Boston, Atlantic, Little, Brown. (c. 1942, 1955).

One reference to the *Historia general...* on p. 125.

256. Morison, Samuel Eliot. *Journals & Other Documents on the Life & Voyages of Christopher Columbus. Translated & Edited by...* New York, Heritage Press, 1963.

Several references to the Ríos edition of *Historia general...* in notes.

257. Moses, Bernard. *Spanish Colonial Literature in South America.* New York-London, The Hispanic Society of America, 1922.

The biographical sketch on pp. 41 — 48 apparently derives from Ríos. On pp. 51 — 54 he presents contrasting accounts of the operation of pearl fisheries from Las Casas and from Oviedo.

258. Muñoz, Juan Bautista. *Historia del Nuevo Mundo.* Madrid, Vda. de Ibarra, 1793. (Only one volume published.)

Great American historian and bibliophile who collected the Oviedo mss now in the collection of the Royal Academy of History which bears his name. Muñoz made extensive use of this material.

259. Muñoz de San Pedro, Miguel. «Francisco Lizaur, hidalgo indiano de principios del siglo xvi.» *Boletín de la Real Academia de la Historia.* XXXIII. Madrid, 1948. pp. 57-170.

Interesting account of a gentleman who preceded Oviedo to the Indies and traveled widely in them prior to his death in 1535. Our chronicler mentions him at least twice.

260. O'Gorman, Edmundo. *The Invention of America.* Indianapolis, Indiana niversity Press, 1961.

For a discussion of Oviedo's interpretation of Columbus' enterprise see pp. 13-20. Also the same author's earlier *La invención de América.* México, Fondo de Cultura Económica, [1958].

261. Olivera, Otto. *Breve Historia de la literatura antillana.* México, Manuales Studium -7, 1957.

Refers to Oviedo only in terms of the *Historia general...*: «Su defecto principal lo constituye el desorden de la narración; pero esto se atenúa un tanto por el vigor que le prestan la espontaneidad y sencillez del estilo. Aunque Oviedo no parece tener muy buena opinión del aborigen americano, lamenta su suerte y censura la codicia y crueldad del conquistador.» pp. 9-10.

262. Orti Belmonte, Miguel Angel. «Páginas de la historia del Gran Capitán.» *Boletín de la Real Academia de Córdoba de Ciencias, Bellas Letras y Nobles Artes.* XXIV (69 - 1953 [1955]) pp. 159-196.

Suggests Oviedo as the possible author of an anonymous «Crónica manuscrita... del Gran Capitán.»

263. Otte, Enrique. «Aspiraciones y actividades heterogéneas de Gonzalo Fernández de Oviedo, cronista.» *Revista de Indias.* XVIII. 71. pp. 9-62.

Study of financial transactions involving Oviedo, especially during the period 1514-1532, based on documents in the Archivo General de Indias.

264. Otte, Enrique. «Una carta inédita de Gonzalo Fernández de Oviedo.» *Revista de Indias.* XVI. 65. Pp. 437-458.

Letter to Prince Philip, dated Santo Domingo, April 12, 1554.

265. Otte, Enrique. «Documentos inéditos sobre la estancia de Gonzalo Fernández de Oviedo en Nicaragua, 1527-1529.» *Revista de Indias.* XVIII. Pp. 627-651.

266. Otte, Enrique. «Gonzalo Fernández de Oviedo und Kaiser Karl über die sustaende in Santo Domingo.» *Spanische Forschungen der Goerresgesellschaft.* Reihe, 11. Bd. S. 165-167.

267. Otte, Enrique. «Gonzalo Fernández de Oviedo y los genoveses. El primer registro de Tierra Firme.» Revista de Indias XXII. 89-90. Pp. 515-519.

The chronicler's friendship with Franco Leardo, prominent Genovese merchant of Seville.

268. Padilla, Lorenzo. «Crónica de Felipe I, llamado el hermoso.» In *Colección de documentos inéditos para la historia de España.* VIII. Madrid, [*Imp.* Vda. de Calero?], 1846.

See p. 112 for an account of French withdrawal from Salsas, Oct. 20, 1503, which Oviedo says he witnessed personally.

269. Palencia, Alonso de. *Crónica latina de Enrique IV.* Tr. A. Paz y Melia. Madrid, Tip. Revista de Archivos, 1905. 4 vols.

Cf. pp. 282-283, Vol. IV, for fate of the Juan de Oviedo, partisan of «la Beltraneja», whom some investigators have supposed was our chronicler's father.

270. Palm, Erwin Walter. *Los monumentos arquitectónicos de la Española.* Ciudad Trujillo, Pub. de la Universidad, Santo Domingo, 1955. 2 vols.

References to Oviedo on pp. 31 and 158 of Vol. I. The latter cites his refusal to pay assessment for repair of city walls on the grounds of *hidalguía.*

271. Palm. Erwin Walter. *...Rodrigo de Liendo, arquitecto de la Española...* Ciudad Trujillo, R. D., Editorial La Nación, 1944.

Quotes from the *Historia general...* concerning construction of the first chapel in Santo Domingo in 1509.

272. Palomeque Torres, Antonio. «Ambiente político y científico que rodeó al futuro Almirante de Indias, D. Cristóbal Colón, en la España de los Reyes Católicos.» [in *Studi Colombiani*, Genoa, SAGA, 1952. Vol. II, pp. 303-356.]

Draws on *Quincuagenas* (or *Batallas y quincuagenas?*) for picture of life at the Spanish court.

273. Parks, George B. «Ramusio's Literary History.» *Studies in Philology* (Chapel Hill), III, 2: pp. 124-148.

Mentions Ramusio's relationship with Oviedo.

274. Pastells, Pablo. *El descubrimiento del estrecho de Magallanes.* Madrid, Sucres. de Rivadeneyra, 1920. 2 vols.

275. Paz Julián. «Noticias de Madrid y de las familias de su tiempo por Gonzalo Fernández de Oviedo.» *Revista de la Biblioteca, Archivo y Museo de Madrid.* 55: 1947. pp. 273-332.

Based on unpublished portions of the *Quincuagenas.*

276. Peña y Cámara, José de la. «Contribuciones documentales y críticas para una biografía de Oviedo.» *Revista de Indias. XVII. 69-70:* pp. 603-705.

A major contribution to Oviedan biography, much of it based on hitherto unpublished documents in the archives of Simancas.

277. Pereyra, Carlos. *Historia de la América Española.* Madrid, Editorial Saturnino Calleja [1920-1926]. 8 vols.

Oviedo's *Historia general...* one of sources cited for vols. I & II.

278. Pereyra, Carlos. *Obras completas,* México, Libreros Mexicanos Unidos, S. A. [1960]. 2 vols.

Oviedo mentioned, particularly in the trilogy of works published earlier under titles: *La obra de España en América,* Cartagena-Madrid, Biblioteca Nueva-Artes Gráficas, 1920; *Conquista de las rutas oceánicas,* Madrid, [Imp. Juan Pueyo], 1923; and *Las huellas de los conquistadores,* Madrid, Imp. Juan Pueyo, 1929. All of these are reprinted in vol. II of the present edition which is edited by Lic. Manuel González Ramírez.

279. Pérez de Tudela Bueso, Juan. «Rasgos del semblante espiritual de Gonzalo Fernández de Oviedo. La hidalguía caballeresca ante el nuevo mundo.» *Revista de Indias. XVII.* 69-70: jul.-dic. 1957. Pp. 391-444.

After the appearance of this article Pérez published his brilliant *Estudio preliminar* on the «Vida y escritos de Gonzalo Fernández de Oviedo» which is found on pp. vii-clxxv of vol. I, the Madrid, 1959, edition of the *Historia general...* This incorporates most of the material of the present article, as well as some of that of Peña's complementary study mentioned above.

280. Petrie, Charles. *Philip II of Spain.* New York, E. W. Norton & Company; [c. 1963].

Account of the monarch to whom our chronicler addressed much of his later correspondence.

281. Pfandl, Ludwig. *Juana la Loca.* 6ta ed. Buenos Aires, Espasa-Calpe, 1951.

Palau mentions an edition, Madrid 1943.

282. Picón Salas, Mariano. *De la conquista a la independencia,* México, Fondo de Cultura Económica, [1944].

Oviedo conteruliano de D. Diego Colón, p. 56; alcaide de Santo Domingo, p. 56; la descripción y el inventor de la rareza americana.

283. Porras Barrenechea, Raúl. «Los cronistas de la conquista (Perú).» *Cuadernos* (e), I. 1941: pp. 177-215.

284. Porras Barrenechea, Raúl. «Los cronistas de la conquista: Molina, Oviedo, Gómara y Las Casas.» *Revista de la Universidad Católica Peruana.* IX. 1941. Pp. 235-252.

285. Prescott, William Hickling. *The Conquest of México.* [lst ed. 1843] *The Conquest of Peru.* [lst ed. 1847] New York, The Modern Library, n. d. (ca. 1936).

Since the second and third parts of Oviedo's *Historia general...* were not to see print until the Ríos edition of Madrid 1851-55, it is clear that Prescott could have known the material on Mexico and Peru only through extracts or copies supplied by his correspondents in Madrid. Nevertheless he makes extensive use of Oviedo in both works. On p. 409 of the present edition there is a biographical sketch of our chronicler which is highly critical of his credulity and lack of erudition. Similar criticism is repeated on p. 1161.

286. Prescott, William Hickling. *Ferdinand and Isabella.* [lst ed. 1837] «New and revised edition.» [3rd] Philadelphia, J. B. Lippincott & Co. 1872. 2 vols.

Cites various Oviedo mss. concerning court life under the Catholic Sovereigns. Photograph of a page of *Las quincuagenas,* pp. 209-210, vol. I. Like Ticknor he confuses the *Quincuagenas* and the *Batallas y quincuagenas.*

287. Prescott, William Hickling. *Philip II.* [lst ed., 1855] Philadelphia, J. B. Lippincot & Co., 1874-1882. 3 vols.

288. Pulgar, Hernando del. *Libro de los claros varones de Castilla.* Toledo, Juan Vásquez, 1486.

Oviedo cites this work in *Las quincuagenas...,* may have owned the edition printed at Valladolid by Francisco Fernández de Córdoba in 1514.

289. Pulgar, Hernando del. *Crónica de los Reyes Católicos por su secretario... versión inédita... Juan de Mata Carriazo.* Madrid, Espasa-Calpe, 1943. 2 vols. [vols. V & VI, *Colección de Crónicas Españolas*].

First printed version appears to have been Nebrija's Latin translation (Granada, 1545) which may have found its way into Oviedo's personal library. There was a Spanish version printed at Valladolid by Sebastian Martínez in 1565, another, Zaragoza, 1567, a third, published at Valencia, in 1780. There is also an edition included in vol. LXX of the *Biblioteca de Autores Españoles.* See p. 64 of the Carriazo edition here cited.

290. Quintana, Jerónimo de la. *A la muy antigua, noble y coronada villa de Madrid. Historia de su antigüedad, nobleza y grandeza.* Madrid, Imprenta del Reyno, 1629.

291. Ramos, Demetrio. «Las ideas de Fernández de Oviedo sobre la técnica de la colonización en América.» *Cuadernos hispano-americanos* (México), 32 (96). Pp. 279-289. dic. 1957.

292. Rassow, Peter and Fritz Schalk, eds. *Karl V. Der Kaiser und seine Zeit.* Cologne, Böhlau Verlag, 1960.

Collection of 16 papers presented at a symposium in Cologne in 1958. See especially Lewis Hanke's «The Other Treasure from the Indies.» (Pp. 94-103) on historical documents.

293. Restrepo Tirado, Ernesto. *De Gonzalo Ximénez de Quesada a don Pablo Morillo...*, París, Le Moil & Pascaly, 1928.

294. Restrepo Tirado, Ernesto. *Historia de la provincia de Santa Marta.* Seville, Eulogio de las Heras, 1929. 2 vols.

295. Rey, Agapito. «Book XX of Oviedo's *Historia general y natural de las Indias.*» *Romanic Review.* XVIII. pp. 52-57.

Rey describes an edition of which he believes to be earlier than the Valladolid printing by Francisco Fernández de Córdoba, 1557, commonly assumed to be the first.

296. Richman, Irving Berdine. *The Spanish Conquerors...* New Haven, Yale University Press, 1919.

On pp. 80-82 cites Oviedo regarding Pedrarias. The reference appears second-hand.

297. Rivet, Paul. «L'Element Blanc et les Pygmées en Amérique.» in: *Procedings of the Thirty-Second International Congress of Americanists.* Copenhagen, Munkegaard, 1958. pp. 587-593.

See references on p. 589 and in Note on 591.

298. Robertson, William. *History of America.* London-Edinburgh, T. Cadell-J. Balfour, 1777. (Consulted in «The First [sic] American from the Tenth London Edition,» Lancaster-Philadelphia, William Geer, 1802), 2 vols.

This enormously popular work which enjoyed numerous reprints in English, French, Spanish and other languages cites Oviedo as one of the oldest historians of the Spanish conquest, apparently on basis of the *Sumario* and first part of *Historia general...* only.

299. Robertson, William. *The History of the Reign of the Emperor Charles V.* Philadelphia, Robert Bell, 1770. 3 vols. (Consulted in printing by J. B. Lippincott Company, Philadelphia, editions of 1856, 74 & 1884. Added «...An account of the Emperor's life after his abdication by William H. Prescott...»:

300. R[odríguez]-Navas [y Carrasco], M[anuel]. «Del cronista Oviedo.» *Cultura Hispano-Americana. III.* Madrid, 1915. pp. 18-23.

Quotation from prolog of the *Sumario...* and some rather naïve pseudo-philological observations on Oviedo's spelling.

301. Rodríguez Villa, Antonio, ed. *Crónicas del Gran Capitán.* Madrid, Bailly, Balliére e Hijos, 1908. [*Nueva Biblioteca de Autores Españoles, X*].

Extracts from the *Batallas...* p. lxviii. See also Pp. 250-265, 463. Peña has pointed out that it is improbable that Oviedo ever knew the Gran Capitán in Italy as Rodríguez assumes.

302. Román de Sirgado, Manuel. *La antropofagia en la zona circumcaribe.* Memoria de Licenciatura. Madrid, 1957.

Unpublished study cited by Ballesteros Gaibrois.

303. Romoli, Kathleen. *Balboa of Darien.* New York, Doubleday & Company, Inc. 1953. (Spanish translation, Madrid, Espasa-Calpe, 1955; French, Paris, 1961).

For evaluation of Oviedo as a source see pp. x-xi. Consult index for numerous references.

304. Rossi, Ettore. «Scritti Turchi su Cristoforo Colombo e la scoperta dell' America.» in *Studi Colombiani*, Genova, SAGA, 1952. Vol. II, pp. 563-66.

In light of Oviedo's statement that the first part of his *Historia general*... had been translated into Turkish the following is of interest: «L'opera a stampa più antica in lingua turca in cui si parla dell'America è la *Ta'rikh-i Hind-i gharbi yakhod hadith-i nev* 'Storia dell' India Occidentale o nuovo racconto di anonimo' composto sotto Murad III all fine del sec. XVI, publicata con figure e disegni a Constantinópli nel 1142/ 1729-30 E. una raccolta di notizie favolose di varia fonte... dipende da fonti scritti europee, specialmente da quelle stampate a Venezia nella seconda metà del sec. XVI...».

305. Salas, Alberto M., ed. *El areito*. [Buenos Aires], Gulab y Aldaba, 1949. [Cuadernos del Eco, III].

Selections from Oviedo, Peter Martyr, Las Casas and López de Gómara.

306. Salas, Alberto M. *Las armas de la conquista*. Buenos Aires, Emecé, 1950.

Oviedo is the authority for description of certain Indian weapons.

307. Salas, Alberto M. «Fernández de Oviedo, crítico de la conquista y de los conquistadores.» *Cuadernos Americanos*. 74 : 2. marzo-abril, 1954. pp. 160-170.

The chronicler as a critic of his compatriots as well of the Indians.

308. Salas, Alberto M. «Fernández de Oviedo y la naturaleza de las Indias.» *Sur*. 211-212. 1952. pp. 111-118.

309. Salas, Alberto M. «Pedro Mártir y Oviedo ante el hombre y las culturas americanas.» *Imago mundi*. I (1953), 2: pp. 16-33.

310. Salas, Alberto M. *Tres cronistas de Indias: Pedro Mártir, Fernández de Oviedo, y Las Casas*.. México, Fondo de Cultura Económica, 1959.

Valuable comparative study. Oviedo treated on pp. 63-160. The final pages of this section catalog Oviedo's principal sources.

311. [Salazar y Castro, Luis, *Cronista mayor de España e Indias*]. *Juicio que de la dedicatoria de la traducción de la Carta de Guía de casados hizo la curiosidad de un ocioso...* Salamanca, Vicente de Senosiain, 1724.

The *Defensa crítica...*, reply to the above of the same year, cites Oviedo concerning Cobos.

312. Sánchez, Luis Alberto. *Nueva historia de la literatura americana.* Buenos Aires, Editorial Americalee, (Col. 1944).

Oviedo mentioned as a poet in brief and inaccurate sketch based on Menéndez Pelayo. (Pp. 31 & 36).

313. Sánchez-Albornoz y Mendina, Claudio. *España, enigma histórico.* Buenos Aires, Editorial Sudamericano, [1962] (1st ed. 1956). 2 vols.

A lengthy refutation of the viewpoint expressed by Américo Castro in his *España en su historia*. No notes or bibliography, but the author shows familiarity with both the *Historia general...* and the *Respuesta a la epístola moral del Almirante...* There are a couple of tantalizingly vague allusions to evaluations of Oviedo by third parties, e. g. his worth as a naturalist, by «Parodi» [Domingo? Lorenzo? Rodolfo?] and his contribution to the study of human geography by «García-Miranda».

314. Sánchez Valverde, Antonio. *Idea del valor de la Isla Española.* Ciudad Trujillo, R. D., Editorial Montalvo, 1947 (1st ed. Madrid, 1785).

See index for the some two dozen references to Oviedo.

315. Santa Cruz, Alonso de. *Islario general de todas las islas del mundo.* Madrid, Imp. del Patronato de Huérfanos de Intendencia e Intervención Militares, 1918-1920. 2 vols.

This work, which cites the *Historia general...* must have been concluded between 1556 and the author's death in 1567 as it addressed to King Philip II. Although there seem to have a number of ms. copies extant it was not printed until the present century.

316. Santiago, Miguel. «Colón en Canarias.» *Anuario de Estudios Atlánticos.* I (Madrid-Las Palmas), 1955. Pp. 337-396.

Draws on Oviedo, Fr. Pedro de Aguado and Fernando Colón.

317. Sauer, Carl O. «Age and Area of American Cultivated Plants.» in *Actas del XXXIII Congreso Internacional de Americanistas,* San José de Costa Rica, Lehman, 1959.

Sauer is apparently unaware of Oviedo's contribution to American agricultural history.

318. Sauer, Carl O. «Maize into Europe.» in *Akten des 34 Internationalen Amerikanistenkongresses. Wien, 1962.* Vienna, Ferdinand Berger, Horn, 1962. Pp. 777ff.

Maintains pre-Colombian introduction of maize into Europe, apparently on the strength of Peter Martyr's use of the word *panicum* (millet) to describe this grain. Ignores Oviedo's evidence that it came from New World.

319. Schäfer, Ernesto. *Indices de documentos inéditos de Indias.* Madrid, Consejo Superior de Investigaciones Científicas, 1946-47. 2 vols.

Indices to both first and second series of the great *Colección de documentos inéditos...* listed above. Numerous references to Oviedo.

320. Schoenrich, Otto. *The Legacy of Christopher Columbus.* Glendale, Cal., The Arthur H. Clark Company, 1949. 2 vols.

A lawyer's fascinating account of the «pleitos de Colón». Numerous references to Oviedo. Illustrations include a photo of the «fortaleza de Santo Domingo» which our Alcaide commanded.

321. Sepúlveda, Juan Ginés de. *De rebus Hispanorum gestis ad Novem Orbem...* [*Opera...*, Vol. III]. Madrid, Real Academia de la Historia, 1780.

According to Sánchez Alonso this Latin work contains summary of unspecified parts of the *Historia general...* Sepúlveda, like Oviedo, was one of the official chroniclers and his contemporary. Aubrey F. G. Bell in his biography tells us that the *De rebus gestis ad Novem Orbem...* was not printed until after Sepúlveda's death in 1573.

322. Serrano y Sanz, Manuel. *Orígenes de la dominación española en América.* Madrid, Bailly Bailliere, 1918. [*Nueva Biblioteca de Autores Españoles,* XXV].

The section entitled «preliminares del gobierno de Pedrarias Dávila en Castilla del Oro» (Pp. [cclix-cccxxxiii] not only cites Oviedo, but reproduces documents dating from 1513 concerning his appointments in Tierra-Firme and his preparations for travel as agent of the Secretary Conchillos.

323. Simpson, Leslie Byrd. *The Encomienda in New Spain...* Berkeley, University of California Press, 1929.

Oviedo cited on early settlers in Hispaniola (pp. 25-26) and Las Casas' failure at Cumaná (p. 143).

324. Steffen, Max. *Die Landwirtschaft bei den altamerikanischen Kulturvölkern.* Leipzig, Dunker & Humblot, 1883.

One of sources cited by Weber for his biographical sketch of Oviedo (pp. 71 ff.).

325. Steward, Julián H. *Handbook of South American Indians. Vol. IV. The Circum-Caribbean Tribes,* Washington, Government Printing Office, 1948.

Illustrations taken from Oviedo reproduced on p. 532.

326. Tapia y Rivera, Alejandro, ed. *Biblioteca histórica de Puerto Rico...* San Juan de Puerto Rico, Imprenta Mayaguez, 1854.

Reproduces portions of the *Historia general...* dealing with Puerto Rico.

327. Taylor, Douglas MacRae. *The Black Carib of British Honduras* New York, Wenner-Gren Foundation, 1951.

Oviedo listed as one of sources.

328. Tejera, Emiliano. *ed.* '«Privilegio y aumento de armas' de G. F. de O.» *Ateneo.* 18: (Santo Domingo, June, 1911).

Document reproduced elsewhere, v. g. Miralles Imperial.

329. Ternaux-Compans, H. *Voyages, Relations et Mémoires originaux pour servir à l'histoire de la découverte de l'Amérique...* Paris, A. Bertrand, 1837-1841. 20 vols.

Vol. IV of 1st series contains a French translation of Xeres' *Conquista del Perú* made from the Salamanca 1547 edition. Vol. IV 2nd series contains the *Histoire de Nicaragua,* mentioned above, which is a translation of part of the *Historia general...*

330. Ternaux-Compans, H. ed. *Recueil des documents et mémoires...* Paris, Gide, 1840.

The section «Moeurs et coutumes des habitants de la province de Cueba» is a translation from the *Historia general...*

331. Ticknor, George. *History of Spanish Literature.* New York, Harper and Brothers, 1849.

Like Prescott confuses the *Quincuagenas* and *Batallas y quincuagenas...* (v. pp. 559-562).

332. Trevor-Davies, R. *The Golden Century of Spain 1501-1621...* London, Macmillan, 1958.

Valuable for study of historical background although there is no mention of Oviedo.

333. Turner, Daymond. «Biblioteca Ovetense: A Speculative Reconstruction of the Library of the First Chronicler of the Indies.» *Papers of the Bibliographical Society of America.* LVII (2). Pp. 157-83.

Identification by title and author of some 119 works mentioned in the *Historia general...* which may have formed part of the alcaide's personal library.

334. Turner, Daymond. «Oviedo's *Claribalte*: The First American Novel.» *Romance Notes.* V (1). Pp. 65-68.

On basis of the author's statement that it was written «mas largamente estando yo en la Yndia», Claribalte merits consideration as the first Spanish-American novel although the American theme is nowhere present in it.

335. Turner, Daymond. «Oviedo's *Historia general y natural de las Indias...* First American Encyclopedia.» *Journal of Inter-American Studies.* V (2). Pp. 267-274.

Because of its nature and scope the *Historia general...* is more of an encyclopedia than a history.

336. Uría Ríu, Juan. «Nuevos datos y consideraciones sobre el linaje asturiano del historiador de las Indias Gonzalo Fernández de Oviedo.» *Revista de Indias.* LXXXI-II (1960). Pp. 13-28.

Cites document discovered at Salamanca which apparently resolves the enigma of our cronista's paternity. His father was one Miguel de Sobrepeña, householder of Borondes, consejo de Grado, province of Asturias. This explains the «alias Sobrepeña» after Oviedo's name on title-page of the *Claribalte...*

337. Utrera, Fr. Cipriano de. *Dilucidaciones históricas.* Santo Domingo, [imprint not given], 1927.

Contains identification of Oviedo's third wife as Catalina de Ribaflecha y Burguillos.

338. Utrera, Fr. Cipriano de. «Isabel la católica, fundadora de la ciudad de Santo Domingo.» *Clío.* XIX (91) 1951. Pp. 116-132.

Compares accounts of foundation of city given by Oviedo and Las Casas, believes that neither is entirely accurate. Printed separately by Tip. Franciscana, Ciudad Trujillo, 1952.

339. Valbuena Prat, Angel. *Historia de la literatura española. Cuarta edición.* Barcelona, Editorial Gustavo Gili, S. A., 1953. 3 vols.

«Gonzalo Fernández de Oviedo es un hábil observador y anotador... La ingenua descripción de costumbres de los indios y las observaciones amenas y graciosas —para el lector de hoy— sobre los animales indígenas, indican condiciones de estilo y simpatía de expresión, algo menos popular que en Bernal Díaz, también menos jugosas, pero de indudable amenidad. 'Oviedo —dice Sánchez Alonso— es la antítesis del humanista. Por eso rechaza el uso del latín... Le importan la veracidad y la exactitud, el valor del testigo de vista, los detalles y las circunstancias, la rica experiencia, la ingenua sencillez...'»
Valbuena mentions the *Batallas y quincuagenas*, the *Historia general...*, the *Sumario...* and a volume of selections edited by M. Ballesteros. (Vol. I, Pp. 452-253.)

340. Vaseo, M. Juan. *Chronici rerum memorablilium Hispaniae tomus prior...* Salamanca, Juan de Junta, 1552.

Harrisse cites a reference to Oviedo on fol. v.

341. Vazquez Vera, Josefina Zoraida. *La imagen del indio en el español del siglo xvi.* Xalapa, Universidad Veracruzana, 1962.

For discussion of Oviedo's attitude towards the Indian see especially Chapter II (Pp. 47-72) and Chapter V (Pp. 122-132).

342. Vazquez Vera, Josefina Zoraida. *El indio americano y su circunstancia en la obra de Oviedo.* Mexico, Universidad Nacional Autónoma, 1956.

Reprinted the following year in *Revista de Indias.* XVII 69-70, jul.-dic. 1957. Pp. 483-520.

343. Vega Bolaños, Andrés, ed. *Colección Somoza. Documentos para la historia de Nicaragua.* Madrid, 1954. 7 vols.

See Vol. I, pp. 154 ff concerning Oviedo's brother-in-law, Diego de Salcedo.

344. Verlinden, Charles. «Santa María la Antigua del Darien: Première 'Ville' Coloniale du Continent Américain.» in *Procedings of the thirty-second International Conference of Americanists.* Copenhagen, Munksgaard, 1958.

Announcement of an expedition to determine the site of Santa Maria, results of which are reported in article below.

345. Verlinden, Charles *et al.* «Santa Maria la Antigua del Darien première 'ville' coloniale de la Terre Ferme américaine...» *Revista de Historia de América* XLV (June 1958). Pp. 1-48.

Description of the results of the Belgian expedition which in early 1956 attempted to established the site of Oviedo's first American station.

346. Vila, Pablo. «Valor geográfico de las crónicas e historias coloniales.» *Boletín de la Sociedad Geográfica de Colombia.* XLI. Pp. 45-56.

347. Wagner, Henry Raup. «Peter Martyr and his works.» *Procedings of the American Antiquarian Society. LVI.* Worcester, Mass. 1947. Pp. 239-288.

Wagner believes that Oviedo knew only the first four decades of *Orbe Novo.*

348. Wagner, Henry Raup. «Three Studies on the Same Subject: Bernal Díaz del Castillo; Notes on Writings by and about Bernal Díaz del Castillo.» *Hispanic American Historical Review.* XXV. Durham, N. C., 1945. Pp. 155-211.

Suggests that Díaz's account of Grijalva expedition may derive from Oviedo.

349. Weber, Friedrich. *Beiträge zur Charakteristik der älteren Geschichtsschreibern: über Spanisch-Amérika. Eine biographisch-bibliographische Skizze...* Leipzig, R. Voigtlander Verlag, 1911.

References to Oviedo on pp. 5, 11, 12, 18, 59, 70, 75, 77, 79, 81, 88, 129, 164, 173, 219, 245, 246, 248, 249 and in note 50. The biographical sketch on pp. 42-47 apparently is based largely on Berìstáin de Souza and Harrisse.

350. Wilgus, Curtis A. *Colonial Hispanic America.* Washington, D. C., The George Washington University Press, 1936.

«Among the earliest and most frequently quoted of the histories concering America... is that of Gonzalo Fernández de Oviedo y Valdés» (p. 573).

351. Wilmer, Lambert A. *The Life, Travels and Adventures of Ferdinand de Soto, Discoverer of the Mississippi.* Philadelphia, [Imprint not given], 1858.

On pages 3 & 4 mentions that 30 books of Oviedo's *Historia general...* remain unpublished. (Hence Wilmer must have had access to the Rangel diary or extracts from it in mss. Actually the last volume of the Ríos adition had appeared three years before present volume was printed.)

352. Williamson, James A. *The Voyages of the Cabots...* London, The Argonaut Press, 1929.

Oviedo quoted in translation on pp. 105-106 concerning John Rut's expedition.

353. Winsor Justin. *Christopher Columbus.* Boston & New York, Houghton Mifflin, 1892.

«In coming to Oviedo we encounter a chronicler who, as a writer, possesses an art far from skillful. Muñoz laments that his learning is not equal to his diligence. He finds him of little service for the time of Columbus and largely because he was neglectful of documents and pursued uncritical combinations of tales and truths. With all his vagueness he is a helpful guide... He was intelligent if not learned, and a power of happy judgements served him in good stead... His opportunities for knowing the truth were exceptional...» (Pp. 38-39). See also pp. 17, 160, 251.

354. Ximénez de Sandoval, Felipe. *Cristóbal Colón.* Madrid. Ediciones Cultura Hispánica, 1953.

Cites 1535 and 1537 editions of the *Historia general...* and Vascosan's French translation of 1555.

355. Zavala Collan, Agustín. «El picaflor en las antiguas crónicas de América.» *Anales de la Asociación Folklórica Argentina.* (Buenos Aires). II. 1946. Pp. 79-83.

Notes and comentaries based on works of Sahagún, Garcilaso el Inca, Fernández de Oviedo, Acosta, *et al.*

www.ingramcontent.com/pod-product-compliance
Lightning Source LLC
Chambersburg PA
CBHW020422230426
43663CB00007BA/1274